SCOTS CONFESSION

1560

edited with an Introduction
by the late Very Reverend
G. D. HENDERSON DD DLitt
Professor of Ecclesiastical History, Aberdeen University
Master of Christ's College

together with a rendering
into modern English by the Reverend
JAMES BULLOCH PhD

SAINT ANDREW PRESS
EDINBURGH

First published in 1960 by
SAINT ANDREW PRESS
121 George Street
Edinburgh EH2 4YN

ISBN 978 0 7152 0843 4

British Library Cataloguing in Publication Data
A catalogue record for this book is available from the British Library

It is the Publisher's policy to only use papers that are natural and recyclable
and that have been manufactured from timber grown in renewable, properly
managed forests. All of the manufacturing processes of the papers are expected
to conform to the environmental regulations of the country of origin.

Typeset by Waverley Typesetters, Fakenham
Printed and bound in the United Kingdom by Bell & Bain Ltd, Glasgow

CONTENTS

PREFACE TO THE 1960 EDITION

In 1937, the Committee on Publications of the Church of Scotland, considering that such a characteristic Reformation document as the *Scots Confession* of 1560 should be easily accessible to members of the Church and other friends, published an edition edited by the late Very Rev. G. D. Henderson DD DLitt. Previously, this Confession was only to be found embedded in large works such as Laing's edition of Knox's writings or Calderwood's eight-volume *History*; and, while scholars had no difficulty in finding them and obtaining all needful information with regard to variant readings and so on, there was a want of a handy edition for the general public.

The edition produced twenty-three years ago is long out of print, and the present volume is issued in view of the celebration of the fourth centenary of the Scottish Reformation. Apart from this special reason, the publication seems justified, for a document which has played such an important part in our Scottish history, and which reveals so plainly the earnest mind of Knox and those who followed him, the fears that beset them and the faith that upheld them, deserves to have wider publicity than has been given it. It is much more inspiring to turn directly to such original records than merely to know their names and read about them. The difference is like that between visiting a place and merely seeing it marked upon the map. Our faithful people ought to know something at first hand about the beginnings of the Reformed Church in Scotland.

The Scots text is here reprinted as in P. Schaff, *The Creeds of the Evangelical Protestant Churches* (1877), following W. Dunlop, *A Collection of Confessions of Faith, Catechisms, Directories, Books of Discipline, &c., of Public Authority in the Church of Scotland* (1719–22), which is based upon the Scots version in Sir John Skene's *Acts of the Parliament of Scotland, 1424–1597* (1597). The Scots text may also be found in several contemporary editions and in D. Laing's edition of *The Works of John Knox* (1845); D. Calderwood's *History of the Kirk of Scotland* (Wodrow Society, 1842); *Acts of Parliament of Scotland, Vol. II* (1814); *Acts of Parliament of Scotland, 1424–1707* (revised edition, 1908); Edward Irving, *Confessions of Faith ... of the Church of Scotland before 1647* (1831) and so on. Most of the editions differ very considerably in spelling; the footnotes in Laing are the best guide in this matter. The few difficulties of text which occur are also discussed there.

The Publishers are grateful to the Rev. James Bulloch PhD for producing at very short notice his rendering of the *Confessio Scoticana* into modern English.

INTRODUCTION

The *Scots Confession* of 1560 embodies the true spirit of our Scottish Reformers. It is a simple, straightforward, frank document, stating in plain language their general credal position, and revealing conviction, determination and enthusiasm. In it, our national religion, from an attitude of mere protest, passed to being positively articulate. It has been described by Lorimer as 'the warm utterance of a people's heart'.

Reformation doctrine began to find acceptance in Scotland almost as early as anywhere, for the condition of the Church was at least as unsatisfactory there as in other countries, and the renaissance of learning and the changing economic conditions of the world affected even this border land of European civilisation. Tyndale's Bible was smuggled into the ports; students such as Patrick Hamilton imbibed the new ideas abroad; Sir David Lyndsay openly satirised the weaknesses of the clergy; and George Wishart was the most outstanding of a band of martyrs who did much to prepare the way.

The Reformation, however, was not finally established until 1560, when at last with singular unanimity and heartiness the nation came to its decision. It was the leadership of John Knox that settled matters in the end.

One of the first steps taken by the Parliament of 1560 was to commission certain of the prominent ministers to produce a statement of the Protestant Christian faith. The result was the *Scots Confession*, officially adopted on 17 August 1560 as 'hailsome and sound doctrine groundit vpoune the infallibill trewth of Godis word'.

Knox himself has told the story in his vivid way, declaring that the document was ready within four days from the time when the order for it was given, that it was first read to the executive of Parliament, and then to the whole House, including representatives of the displaced ecclesiastical system. No objections were stated. A few days later, each article was read over once more, and the vote taken. Knox names three nobles who insisted that they would believe as their fathers had done, and indicates that the bishops kept quiet. It is also from Knox that we learn how the Confession was the work of six men with a common Christian name – John Winram, John Spottiswood, John Douglas, John Row, John Willock and John Knox.

We can check his narrative by other contemporary accounts. The English ambassador sent a copy of the Confession to his Government, and expressed his astonishment at the speed and cordiality with which this important business had been dispatched. He stated that the lords of the Articles heard Knox and Willock in explanation of the Confession before it came before Parliament. The two nobles whom he mentions as voting against the Confession are not in Knox's list of three, and he attributes to one of the bishops a long speech (in which he was supported by two others) to the effect that there had not been time to examine the document and that, while he would not therefore vote against it, neither could he consent to it. We are told on the other hand how one venerable nobleman fervently praised God that he had lived to see that day, and how others eagerly and devoutly declared their adherence to the new statement of doctrine. We gather that the Englishman thought the Scottish Reformers very uncompromising; but he also indicates that Lethington and Winram softened some of the expressions in the original draft of the Confession, and sought (though apparently without success) to have the article on the Civil Magistrate, or part of it, suppressed. It would seem that the first version of the document was the work of one man, and we can only suppose this to have been Knox.

Maitland of Lethington, in a letter to England, refers in passing to the heartiness of the reception of the Confession, and mentions that it had the approval of the great majority of the clergy.

Ministers were in readiness to expound any difficult point of doctrine that might be raised in Parliament, but the laymen present had neither the knowledge nor the interest for a theological discussion. They were out for reformation, and the dogmatic implications they were prepared to leave to their prophets. The attitude of the non-reforming clergy is not so easy to explain. Bellesheim, the Romanist historian, admits that their non-resistance 'appears difficult altogether to justify'. Public opinion was, of course, clearly against them. They were only too well aware of the abuses responsible for the upturn. It was obvious that the nobles were ready to be provoked into plundering. Even the leading clergy were neither of the martyr type nor theologians and Bible scholars. And possibly they did not realise that the end had come, and looked forward to a speedy reversal of the proceedings. A letter from Scotland addressed to John Calvin in September 1560 is of some interest with regard to the clerical position. It is not surprising that some, like the Earl Marischal, found support and encouragement for their Protestantism in the failure of the Romanists to make any stand on this occasion.

The *Scots Confession*, after its adoption, quickly appeared in print. Already in 1561, three editions (Lekprewik, Edinburgh; Scot, Edinburgh; and Rowland Hill, London) were published. A useful Latin translation, attributed to Patrick Adamson, the scholarly but unfortunate Archbishop of a later period, was issued in 1572.

Queen Mary, not unnaturally, withheld her royal approval from the doctrinal revolution carried through by a Parliament whose acts she regarded as irregular as well as undesirable, and it was not until 1567 that the *Scots Confession* was constitutionally ratified by the first Parliament of the infant James VI, and 'authorisit as a doctrine groundit upon the infallibil Worde of God'.

*   *   *   *   *

One of the most interesting features of the *Scots Confession* is the plainness with which in the Preface it avows its anxiety to accord in all respects with the Word of God. In similar fashion, the *First Book of Discipline* (1560), which came from the same hands, declared that it claimed acceptance only in so far as its requirements could be substantiated from 'God's plain Scriptures'.

A multitude of passages in Knox's *Works* bear witness how completely he relied upon the authority of the Bible. This was no mere individual opinion of his own. On a critical occasion, Andrew Melville, the establisher of Scottish Presbyterianism, 'clanked' his Bible down on the table before King and Council and declared: 'Thair is my instructiones and warrand'. Nor was it a peculiarity of the Scottish Reformation. The *First Confession of Basel* (1534) concludes with the sentence: 'We submit this our Confession to the judgment of the Divine Scriptures, and hold ourselves ready always thankfully to obey God and His Word if we should be corrected out of the said Holy Scriptures'. Rivetus, a celebrated teacher in Holland, wrote indignantly to a Scottish friend in 1617 with reference to the Jesuit suggestion that the Dutch Church by its use of a Confession of Faith had left and quitted the Scriptures. Elsewhere we find him plainly teaching that 'Sacra Scriptura est principium theologiae doctrinae'. One also recalls Article VI of the Thirty-nine Articles. Chillingworth's extreme statement that 'the Bible only is the religion of Protestants' is not without historical foundation.

The *Scots Confession*, following Calvin, denies that the Bible owes its authority to the Church. The Scriptures are 'sufficient to instruct and make the man of God perfite', and contain 'all thingis necessary to be beleeved for the salvation of mankinde'. Interpretation is left to the Holy Spirit, who 'is in nathing contrarious unto himselfe', working in and through the Church.

The Reformers sincerely desired to subordinate their own judgment to Scripture thus divinely interpreted. The difficulties of their position in this respect were not at that date at all obvious. The proof-text method of using the Bible was assumed without discussion, and every doctrinal statement was held to be established by references in connection with which no attention was necessarily paid to context or relevancy, or which involved irresponsible allegorising. There was no awareness of contradictions, no historical sense, no discriminating between temporal and permanent, local and universal, and no consciousness of a subjective element in their understanding of the Word. The *Catholic Encyclopaedia* suggests that the appeal to Scripture was 'practically harmless, for no one ever convinced John Knox that he was in error'; and it is clear to us that the Reformers read their Bibles very definitely with the eyes of Augustine, Luther and Calvin, and were incapable of doing otherwise, or of taking seriously any other interpretation. In the *Scots Confession*, we trace the influence of Calvin's *Institutes* and John à Lasco's *Compendium*; but these were accepted as strictly based upon Scripture. The intention of Knox and his friends was to be utterly scriptural, and to rely completely upon the guidance of the Holy Spirit interpreting the Word.

* * * * *

In connection with the early seventeenth-century Arminian controversy, there was a noticeable tendency on the part of the orthodox to idolise the *Belgic Confession* and the *Heidelberg Catechism*, and to interpret the Bible by these rather than interpret these by the Bible. The same dangerous temptation beset many in Scotland in the eighteenth and nineteenth centuries with respect to the *Westminster Confession*. But those who devised the *Scots Confession* claimed for it no infallibility or finality of expression. The function of a Confession is not to bind but to loose: it should help us to understand and not provide a substitute for understanding; it should be a means and never an end. Like law and like language it should liberate, though too often like these it does the opposite. In Scotland at the Reformation, we discover not only the willingness to alter anything that could be proved unbiblical, but also no hesitation about warmly approving other Protestant utterances, as was in fact done in the case of the *Second Helvetic Confession* (1566). Scots who ministered in French churches signed the *Gallic Confession*. Students in Scottish universities throughout the seventeenth century were instructed in the *Heidelberg Catechism*. And the numerous editions of Knox's *Book of Common Order* all included at the beginning the *Confession of Faith used in the English Congregation at Geneva*. Finally, when the

5

Westminster Confession was introduced in 1647, no difficulty of principle was experienced in accepting a new Confession so long as it could be shown to be in harmony with the *Scots Confession* and in accordance with the Word. Confessions were recognised to be human products; and, while one might and did criticise those of others, one remained deliberately and gladly in communion with them, always under the supreme test of the Word.

It must also be noted that the *Scots Confession* was not regarded as a substitute for, or a denial of, the early Creeds of the undivided Church. The *First Book of Discipline* demands of communicants a knowledge, not of the *Scots Confession*, but of the *Apostles' Creed*. In Knox's *Book of Common Order*, the *Creed* appears in the ordinary Public Worship at the close of one of the prayers, and also in the Baptismal Service. The *Creed* is rehearsed as part of Calvin's *Catechism*, which was declared 'the most perfect that ever yet was used in the Kirk', and is also included in Craig's *Catechism*, the *Heidelberg Catechism* and the 1644 *Catechism for Young Children*. It finds a place, too, in the 1582 form for the election of elders and deacons. In 1604, the Kirk Session of Aberdeen instructed the reader every Sunday to repeat the *Creed* 'that be the oft repeting and hering ... the commoun people may lerne the same perquier' (by heart). The Synod of Fife in 1611 decreed that none might be married unless they knew the *Apostles' Creed*. In 1642, the Session at Culross was threatening with heavy penalties such as could not repeat the *Creed*. A schoolmaster in the Presbytery of Strathbogie in 1637 had to expound the *Apostles' Creed* 'for the tryall of his knowledge of the groundes of religion', and another is recorded as doing the same a few years later after the change from Episcopacy to Presbyterianism. Fraser of Brea, who was born in 1639, tells how his father taught the *Creed* to his family. The *Creed* is printed at the close of the *Shorter Catechism* with a note to indicate that it was not composed by the Apostles and is not canonical Scripture like the Lord's Prayer and Ten Commandments, but 'is a brief summary of the Christian faith, agreeable to the Word of God, and anciently received in the churches of Christ'.

The rehearsal of the *Creed* in the regular services seems to have fallen into disuse among the more puritan ministers even before 1638; and under English influence it came to disappear even in the Baptismal Service, reference to the *Westminster Confession* replacing it here, a practice which was roundly condemned by Episcopalians, the Presbyterians offering in defence such statements as this: 'Neither do we condemn the use of the *Creed*, but we think they who have their children baptized should profess their faith so as may more clearly distinguish them from Popish and other hereticks than that Confession of Faith (the *Creed*) can do'. After the Revolution, the *Creed* had become so closely associated in Scottish minds with the Episcopacy, of which it had lately been one of the few distinctive features, that it may be said to have dropped almost completely out of use – a fact which is emphasised in the malicious *Scotch Presbyterian Eloquence Displayed*. The prejudice has clearly no justification in the practice of our Reformers, which did not in this respect differ from that of the Protestants of England or Geneva.

*   *   *   *   *

Religious instruction in Scotland was chiefly attempted through catechising, and before the days of the *Shorter Catechism* the Church made full use of the Catechisms of Calvin, Beza, Craig and Welsh. But it was the Confession of Faith which formed the test of Reformation orthodoxy. Suspected Romanists were invited to sign the *Scots Confession*. The officers of King's College, Aberdeen, were deprived in 1569 for refusing to sign the *Scots Confession*. The *Book of the Universall Kirk* records cases of persons similarly tested in 1571 and other years. In 1578, the Privy Council was arranging with the Church for the punishment of those suspected of Popery who declined to subscribe the Confession. Presbytery and Synod minutes show examples of the application of such a test. Thus, in 1606 a man is given orders 'that he sall publicklie in the Kirk of Kilmacolme in presence of the congregation subscrybe the Confession of Faith, sware by haulding up his hand in presence of the people that fra his heart he willingly renounces and sall renounce hereafter Papistrie, and sall profess to his lyfe's end the treuth of God for the present publickly preached in Scotland and allowed by his Majesty's laws'. In 1609, someone who had been abroad was required at Aberdeen 'to swear and subscribe to the articles of the Christian fayth and religioun presentlie professit within this realm'.

The *Scots Confession* was indeed a strongly anti-Roman document. This was only natural in the circumstances. Principal Robertson, the historian, says that it was 'composed, as might be expected from such a performance at that juncture, on purpose to expose the absurd tenets and practices of the Roman Church'. We may say that the intention of it was to state the orthodox Catholic doctrine as it continued to be believed in the reformed Church, to the clear exclusion of the corruptions and misunderstandings that had emerged in the unreformed. It was a manifesto of revolt rather than a calm scientific analysis and exposition of the Faith. Like other war-time documents, it breathes little of the spirit of charity and toleration. It is frankly vituperative where its modern counterpart would doubtless be subtly insinuative; but it is no more bitter than are party utterances in our own day, and the *Catholic Encyclopaedia* speaks of it as 'written in a vigorous, original and, for a document proceeding from the pen of Knox, in an extremely moderate style'.

Attention is directed to many Romish errors, to the mistake in all emphasis on human merit and the possibility of works of supererogation and trust in 'damnable idolatry' and so on. The Reformation is not, however, regarded as merely improving here and there upon what had come to be customary in the Church, but as the decisive overthrow of Satan, who had insinuated himself into God's throne and contrived to appropriate the Church's worship to himself and to distort the institution accordingly, so that it had become 'his pestilent synagoge', the 'horrible harlot, the Kirk malignant', whose adherents are 'impudent blasphemers' with an attitude of 'cankred malice'.

It is declared that the true Church is not known by 'antiquitie, title usurpit, lineal descence, place appointed, nor multitude of men approving ane error', but by 'the trew preaching of the Worde', 'the right administration of the Sacraments', and 'ecclesiastical discipline uprightlie ministred'.

There is some emphasis upon the doctrine of the Church invisible, and the individual Church and congregation certainly receive more notice than the universal Church on earth.

The infallibility of Councils is denied. Superstition is strongly condemned. Transubstantiation is declared to have been 'perniciouslie taucht and damnablie beleeved'. The Sacraments are stated to be only two in number, according to Christ's institution. The Zwinglian teaching as to 'naked and baire signes' is in more than one place strongly repudiated, and so also is Anabaptist doctrine with regard to Infant Baptism. It is alleged that the Papists are no true ministers of Christ; and, curiously, one point of evidence for this is found in the permission which had long been granted to women to baptise in emergency. Strong objection is taken to the corruption of the Sacraments by unscriptural additions, such as the use of oil, salt and spittle in baptism, and the veneration and reservation of the elements, the parade of them through the streets, and the refusal of the cup to the laity. The reformers proclaim that they 'abhorre, detest, and renounce' the blasphemous profession of the priest to offer a sacrifice propitiatory for the sins of the quick and the dead as 'making derogation to the sufficiencie' of the one sacrifice of Christ Jesus.

The duty of the civil magistrate includes the maintenance of the true religion and the suppression of idolatry and superstition, but it is made clear that Christ is the only Head of the Church, Sovereign and Supreme Governor. Neither Papal nor Royal head is admitted.

No explicit reference occurs to a number of the outstanding abuses of the pre-Reformation Church. They are left for repudiation to the *First Book of Discipline*, which was the work of the same group who produced the *Scots Confession*, and which must be read along with the Confession if we are to obtain an adequate view of the outlook of the Scottish Reformers.

* * * * *

The *Scots Confession* is neither so carefully complete nor so rigidly systematic as the *Westminster Confession*. It was produced by men who were worried, not so much by the niceties of theological controversy, as by practical problems of the Christian life, worship, government and discipline. It was somewhat hastily put together, though the writers were far from being unprepared for such a task, the Reformation being by this date no new thing, and the documents and practice of other Churches quite familiar. From the scientific point of view, the *Scots Confession* is unsatisfactory on account of repetition, vagueness and imperspicuity.

There is therefore no cause for surprise that the seventeenth century sought, both in the Episcopalian but Calvinistic *Aberdeen Confession* of 1616 and in the *Westminster Confession* of 1647, fuller logical and speculative satisfaction. The *Westminster Confession* was of course adopted in Scotland strictly in the interests of uniformity; but that nothing new or strange in the sphere of doctrine was brought from Westminster is plain from the theological discussions at the Glasgow Assembly in 1638. At the same time, the more scholastic mind of this period desired richer detail than seemed necessary to the Reformers. Westminster delved more laboriously into the problems of Election and Predestination, the imputation of the guilt of Adam, and of the righteousness of Christ, to men, the limitation of the extent of God's purpose in the Atonement, and the condition of Reprobation.

The Calvinism of the *Scots Confession* is undoubted, but is mild and indeterminate as compared with later expressions. The full acceptance of the general body of Christian doctrine is plain, the historical arrangement of the earlier Articles being evidence that the Reformation attempted no departure from the old orthodoxy. At the same time, there are sentences which state with peculiar lucidity some of the special teaching of the Reformation leaders. We have utterances such as these: 'As without Christ Jesus there is nouther life nor salvation, so sal there nane be participant thereof bot sik as the Father hes given unto His Sonne'; 'Of nature we are so dead, so blind, and so perverse, that nether can we feill when we ar pricked, see the licht when it shines, nor assent to the will of God when it is reveiled, unles the spirit of the Lord Jesus quicken that quhilk is dead, remove the darknesse from our myndes, and bowe our stubburne hearts to the obedience of His blessed will'.

One rejoices also in the refusal of the Confession to admit any interpretation of Scripture that offends against 'the rule of charitie' and further, in the sensible declaration that policies and ceremonies are not for all times and places, but may be changed, and ought to be so changed if they threaten to degenerate into mere superstitious formalities.

* * * * *

The *Scots Confession* remained the official doctrinal statement of the Church of Scotland until superseded (though not abrogated) by the adoption of the *Westminster Confession* in 1647. It was thus the Confession upon which were nourished Archbishop Spottiswood, Bishop Patrick Forbes and Archbishop Sharp as well as Andrew Melville, Alexander Henderson, David Dickson and Robert Baillie. All ministers signed this Confession.

There are not very many direct quotations from the Confession in the theological literature of the period, chiefly for the excellent reason that writers usually made their references direct to Scripture. But Robert Bruce appeals to its authority in one of his *Sermons on the Sacraments*. It is used in evidence in more than one connection by the staunch Presbyterian, David Calderwood; and John Forbes of Corse, his Episcopalian adversary, quotes it in several passages of his early *Irenicum* and *Peaceable Warning*, and also in the much later *Instructiones*. There are references to its articles by the Aberdeen Doctors and in the *Large Declaration* of King Charles, as well as in the anti-Roman writings of John Welsh in Scot's *Apologetical Narration*, and in more than one of Samuel Rutherfurd's books, notably his *Lex Rex*. John Menzies in his *Roma Mendax*, written when he was an Episcopalian, quotes in Latin from the 21st Article; the Covenanting *A Hind let loose* quotes Article 14; and there are several allusions in Dr George Garden's *Life* of Forbes. The last-mentioned works belong to the period after the introduction of the *Westminster Confession*, and remind us that the influence of the *Scots Confession* survived that date.

*　　*　　*　　*　　*

After the Restoration, the Rescissory Act deprived the *Westminster Confession* of its still comparatively fresh legal status in Scotland, and by implication restored the *Scots Confession*, so that the latter is mentioned by Bishop Gilbert Burnet as 'the only Confession of Faith that had the sanction of a law'. The Episcopalian author of *The Case of the present afflicted Clergy* (1690) states that 'the Confession of Faith made by Mr Knox and ratified in Parliament by King James VI and renewed again in the Test Act by King Charles II, this, together with the *Westminster Confession* ..., are owned, next to the Word of God, by both parties as the standard of the doctrine of our Church'.

The *Westminster Confession* certainly retained its place in common use under the Second Episcopate, as is clear from such pamphlets as *Some Questions Resolved* (1690), *A Vindication of the Church of Scotland* (1691) and *A brief and true account of the sufferings of the Church of Scotland* (1690). William Forbes, first Bishop of Edinburgh, was indeed as friendly as Laud to Arminianism, and the same might be said of a few more. Professors Strachan and Munro refused to sign the *Westminster Confession* when it was restored to official status at the Revolution Settlement. Leighton and his school were somewhat unsystematic in their Calvinism owing to the influence of Mysticism and Platonism. And doubtless some were of the same mind as Bishop John Sage, who is described as satisfied with neither Calvinists (whom he thought heterodox in many points) nor Arminians (whom he regarded as Trimmers and in danger of Arianism and Socinianism). The great English theologians were widely read – Andrewes and Jeremy Taylor and Stillingfleet and Tillotson as much as Owen and Baxter. But there can be no gainsaying the general acceptance of the *Westminster Confession*, which Burnet tells us was 'the only Confession read in those years in Scotland', having been 'left in possession though the authority that enacted it was annulled'.

* * * * *

Certainly, one does not find very much reference to the *Scots Confession* in those years. Its revival in connection with the Test Act is a curious story. This unfortunate measure was enacted in 1681 to procure the submission of all in Church or State positions to the royal supremacy in temporal and spiritual causes alike, and to obtain from them a repudiation of the Covenants. There was at first no thought of making reference to any particular Confession. That of Westminster had been deposed from its legal position and could not be used. But Dalrymple, President of the Court of Session, knew this *Scots Confession* and liked its strong language against tyrants, while, as Burnet reports, the Confession had become 'so worn out of use that scarcely anyone in the whole Parliament had ever read it; none of the bishops had, as appeared afterwards'. Playing upon the general ignorance, Dalrymple persuaded the authorities to introduce a clause which completely stultified what followed it with regard to the royal supremacy in religious matters: 'That I own and sincerely profess the true Protestant religion contained in the Confession of Faith recorded in the First Parliament of King James VI, and that I believe the same to be founded on and agreeable to the written Word of God'.

Honest clergy promptly examined this *Scots Confession* which they found themselves receiving once more; and though generally, Burnet informs us, 'it was found to be much more moderate in many points than could have been well expected, considering the heat of that time', still the contradiction was discovered, and other objections were raised. The Aberdeen Episcopalians found some passages obscure and doubtful, as where the image of God is declared to be utterly defaced, where the marks of the true Church are enumerated, where the ministers of the pre-Reformation Church are declared not to be true ministers of Christ, where the Confession unchurches such as do not rightly administer the Sacraments or fail to use the appointed elements, where resistance to magistrates is only forbidden conditionally, and where the putting down of tyrants is applauded. Bishop Paterson of Edinburgh said that the *Scots Confession* 'was formed in the infancy of our Reformation and deserves its own praise', but that he could not swear to every clause in it, but only to 'the true Protestant religion founded upon the Word of God contained in that Confession, as it is opposed to Popery and Fanaticism'. While so many Episcopalians protested, the Presbyterians had the prime difficulty of reconciling what the *Scots Confession* had to say of the headship of Christ with what the Test required as to the relation of the King and the Church.

*   *   *   *   *

Passing over for the moment the connection of the *Scots Confession* with the Covenants, we may remind ourselves that there have been some favourable comments upon it in more recent times, especially in the course of criticism of the *Westminster Confession*.

Thus, in the early nineteenth century, Edward Irving, that eccentric genius, described the *Scots Confession* as 'the banner of the Church' in its conflicts, as contrasted with the later 'camp-colours which she hath used during her days of peace'. He read the Confession to his congregation at regular intervals, regarding it as the pillar of the Reformation, 'written in a most honest, straightforward, manly style, without compliment or flattery, without affectation of logical precision and learned accuracy, as if it came fresh from the heart of laborious workmen, all the day long busy with the preaching of the truth and sitting down at night to embody the heads of what was continually taught'. He was much impressed by the doctrine of the Sacraments in the *Scots Confession*, which he credited with saving him from 'the infidelity of evangelicalism, which denies any gift of God either in the work of Christ or in the Sacraments or elsewhere, until we experience it to be within ourselves; making God a mere promiser, until we become receivers ... making religion only subjective in the believer and not elective in God ... a religion of moods and not of purposes and facts, having its reality in the creature, its proposal of reality only in God'. He dismisses this Confession at last 'with the highest encomium which I am capable of bestowing upon a work of fallible man'.

The distinguished theologian, John McLeod Campbell, another rebel from the Westminster standards, frequently turns to the *Scots Confession*. He speaks of it as always having been recognised 'as of authority in the Church', and he was attracted to it specially because it did not deny that Christ died for all men. Both in his *Memorials* (1877) and in *The Whole Proceedings in the Case* (1831), we find quotations and references, which show his anxiety to align himself with Scottish tradition, if not with that of the Covenanters, then at least with what he believed was the position of the Reformers.

Apart from such somewhat partisan praise, much appreciation has been shown by men who would not have cared to return to this earliest of our Confessions. Wodrow avows his preference for the *Westminster Confession*, but calls the other 'an excellent summary of Christian doctrine'. It is commended by theologians so different in outlook as Dr James Walker (*Scottish Theology and Theologians*, 1872), Dr Matthew Hutchison (*Reformed Presbyterian Church in Scotland*, 1893) and Dr Donald Macleod (*Ministry and Sacraments of the National Church of Scotland*, 1903). And the historian, Professor A. F. Mitchell, says: 'We shall not hesitate to own that it holds a distinguished place among the Confessions of that age, and is a credit to our reformer and his associates'. In the Church of Scotland as reunited in 1929, the *Scots Confession* officially finds a place with the *First* and *Second Books of Discipline* and Knox's *Book of Common Order* as a document 'held in honour as having an important place in the history of Scottish Presbyterianism'. It is further of interest that Dr Karl Barth made the *Scots Confession* the basis of his Gifford Lectures at Aberdeen in 1937–8, treating the document 'as a witness to, not as a law of, the Reformed teaching'.

*   *   *   *   *

But we must go back to notice what is in some ways the most interesting association of the *Scots Confession*.

It continued to exercise a certain influence in Scotland even into the eighteenth century among the Reformed Presbyterians, and in the period of the First Secession, through its close connection with the *Negative Confession* of 1581, which in 1638 became the first of the three sections of the *National Covenant*. Into this story we must enter a little more fully.

* * * * *

There was inordinate nervousness in Scotland, about the year 1580, with regard to counter-Reformation influences. One preacher declared that Romanists were swarming home to Scotland 'like locusts'. People were particularly suspicious of the activities of Esmé Stuart, the boy King's favourite at that date. Hume Brown goes so far as to say that Esmé Stuart 'is more responsible than any other single person for the course of Scottish affairs till the Revolution of 1689'. He was an advocate of French absolutism, but he was also, in spite of a hastily adopted profession of Protestantism, popularly regarded as busy with intrigue in favour of Rome. His personal inclinations would probably have led him into Romish propaganda work had not his political existence in Scotland depended upon remaining on good terms with the Reform party.

Suspicion of Stuart led to suspicion of King James, who found it necessary to make an ardent declaration of his adhesion to the Protestant faith. It was commonly believed, as Calderwood tells us, that 'many masked Papists subscribed the old Confession deceitfully'; and Spottiswood hints that these had dispensations from the Pope. No mere renewal of the *Scots Confession* would therefore suffice to allay public fears. The King accordingly commissioned John Craig, one of the most eminent of the preachers and the author of a popular catechism, to frame a short Confession which no Papist could possibly sign.

The result was the *Negative Confession*, sometimes also called the *King's Confession* and the *Second Scottish Confession*, and later often described, rather confusingly, as the *National Covenant*.

Robert Baillie's version of events may be quoted: 'In the year 1580 some prime courtiers and others truly popish in their heart, yet for their own ends was content to dissemble and to abjure popery with their owne equivocations and mentall reservations, the King, desiring to stop all starting holes, caused Mr Craige, the pastor of his familie, to draw up a confession every particular rejecting expressly the most of the Romish errours'.

The original of this Confession in the Scottish National Library bears the King's signature, as well as that of Esmé Stuart and the rest of the Court. The General Assembly accepted it readily as 'a true and Christian Confession to be agreed unto by such as truly profess Christ and his true religion'. Copies were widely distributed and signed, the ecclesiastical authorities having orders to proceed against all 'refusers'. Gilbert Brown, the Romanist controversialist, referred to it as 'their Confession of Faith which they compel all men to swear and subscribe'. It was required of university graduates, and we find it being repeatedly renewed at Court and throughout the land, and printed in every edition of Craig's well-known Catechism.

Row, the Protestant historian, describes it as 'a more particular Confession of Faith than was sett downe at the first', and Calderwood says that it 'is nothing els but the first Confession enlarged with some generall clauses and rejection of Popish errors'.

It is in fact simply a very strongly worded catalogue of what the Protestant in Scotland abhorred and detested and refused in Romish teaching and practice. The *Catholic Encyclopaedia* calls it 'the most violent condemnation of Papistry that ever issued from a Calvinistic pen'. Schaff describes it as 'the most fiercely anti-Popish of all Confessions'; Edward Irving as 'one of the most nervous protestations against the Papacy that was ever penned'; and W. L. Mathieson as 'that exhaustive execration of all things papal'.

An anonymous opponent thought it advisable to issue at once '*Ane schort Catholik Confession of the headis of the religion now controverted in Scotland answering against the heretical Negative Confession set forth be Jhone Craig in his Catechise*'.

*   *   *   *   *

The *Negative Confession* was not entirely negative, for it included definite endorsement of the *Scots Confession*. Those who accepted it declared their adhesion to the true faith and religion as received by the Church of Scotland 'as mair particularlie is expressed in the Confession of our Faith stablished and publickly confirmed by sundrie actis of Parliaments and now of a lang tyme hath been openlie professed by the King's majesty, and haill body of this realme both in brugh and land, to the quhilk Confession and forme of religion we willingly agree in our consciences in all pointis, as unto Godis undoubted trewth and veritie, groundit only upon his written Word'.

All who signed the *Negative Confession* were expressly acknowledging the *Scots Confession* and adding an unequivocal renunciation of Romanism.

When the leaders of the Scottish Church in 1638 sought some means of securing impressive national support for their opposition to King Charles's ecclesiastical programme, they naturally turned to this Covenant and Confession of 1581. It was a document well known to the people and already several times renewed. It had been signed by the King's father, and therefore carried with it no suggestion of disloyalty. It was strongly anti-Roman and so fitted the feelings of Scots at a time when Romanism was intensely feared and when it was suspected in every proposal of Laud. And it was capable of an interpretation which rendered it anti-Episcopal.

To this *Negative Confession* were added a list of recent Acts of Parliament directed against Romanism, and a third section, said to be the work of Alexander Henderson and Johnston of Wariston, by way of application to the circumstances of the moment. This composite document is the famous *National Covenant* first signed at Greyfriars Kirk in Edinburgh on 28 February 1638. The *National Covenant,* with its more political and aggressive companion the *Solemn League and Covenant* of 1643, was of epoch-making importance in Scottish history.

The extraordinary success of the Covenant movement greatly perturbed King Charles. He made desperate efforts to stem the tide that was flowing in Scotland, and issued a declaration that he had himself signed the *Scots Confession* with the 1581 *Negative Confession*, and instructed that this and not the new *National Covenant* was to be accepted by all. A Privy Council proclamation to the same effect followed. This counter-endeavour was a complete failure and even roused dissatisfaction among the Episcopalians in Scotland. The Aberdeen Doctors, the most respected of the anti-Covenanters, disliked the *Negative Confession* and would only sign it with important reservations while declaring their adherence to the *Scots Confession*. One difficulty was the constant assertion of the Presbyterians that the *Negative Confession* was anti-Episcopal. Robert Baillie had doubts on this point, but it was the view of the Glasgow Assembly of 1638, and was frequently affirmed, as, for example, very emphatically by Calderwood in his *History*, and at a later date by *A Vindication of the Church of Scotland* (1691), which states dogmatically that in the *Negative Confession* 'Episcopacy is condemned under the name of the Hierarchy' and 'is abjured'. Dr William Barlow had made out that King James at the Hampton Court Conference in 1604 expressed his distaste for the *Negative Confession* and its long list of 'detestations and abrenunciations', and said that if he were to be bound by such a Confession it would have to be in his table-book and not in his head. In thoughtlessly pressing this Confession upon his friends, Charles was thus putting them in an awkward position and certainly not solving the Scottish problem.

The Covenanting attitude is clear from the minutes of Lanark Presbytery: 'It is thought good by the nobilitie and all degrees of supplicantes that the old Confession of Faith, subscryved dyverse tymes befoir in this Kirke by prince and people, together with an application of it to the present tymes, preveening those many encroaching corruptiones, be drawen upe in form of a Covenant and presented to everie parochin and all degrees of people throughout the land to be subscryved and sworne to by all who loves the truth of the Gospel'.

*   *   *   *   *

All who took the *National Covenant* avowed their acceptance of the *Scots Confession*. This applies not only to the early days of the Covenants but also to the even more exciting times of the persecutions, so that the authority of the *Scots Confession* may be said to have remained alongside that of the *Westminster Confession* among the hillmen and conventiclers and Cameronians. In the Reformed Presbyterian Church, which declined the Revolution Settlement, we find the Covenants renewed at Crawfordjohn in 1712, and more than 100 years later still regarded as of perpetual obligation. And the Associate Presbytery and Synod which resulted from the First Secession of 1733 also insisted upon the renewing of the Covenants and even made the acceptance of these a term or condition of admission to Communion. One reason for their disagreement with George Whitefield in 1741 was his attitude to the Covenants.

It is true that, in the Church of Scotland and in the Relief Church which sprang up in 1761, there was a somewhat different feeling with regard to the Covenants. They had not been enforced at the Revolution Settlement (1690) and were definitely not regarded as of perpetual obligation. There remained, however, and still remain, romantic and sentimental associations about the word Covenanter, and the name must always carry with it a reminder of the first native Confession of the Reformed faith in Scotland.

There is no thought of renewing the Covenants today, and similarly there is no thought of returning to the use of the *Scots Confession*. Both were essentially temporary in character, but they mark experiences in the spiritual history of our race which have helped to make it what it is. We shall not pass that way again, whatever changes may befall us, but we have in fact passed that way; and we shall be none the less able to help our own generation to express its spiritual convictions if we honour the memory and appreciate the efforts of those who, at that great period of advance which we call the Reformation, made such splendid acknowledgement in Scotland of the Sovereignty of God and gave such convincing utterance to the freshest thinking and the deepest moral feeling and the highest spiritual determination of which their age was capable.

The Confessione of the fapht and
doctrin beleued and professed by the
Protestantes of the Realme of Scotland exhibited to the estates of the
sam in parliament and by thare
publict votes authorised as a
doctrin grounded upon
the infallable wourd
of God

Matth. 24.
And this glaid tydinges of the kingdom shalbe preached throught the hole
world for a witness to all nations and
then shall the end cum.

Imprinted at Edinburgh,
be Robert Lekprewik.

Cum priuilegio.
1561.

THE
CONFESSION
OF THE
Faith and Doctrine,

Belevit and professit be the

PROTESTANTIS OF SCOTLAND,

Exhibit to the Estaitis of the same in Parliament, and be their publick Votis authorisit, as a Doctrine groundit upon the infallibil Worde of God, *Aug.* 1560. And afterwards stablished and publicklie confirmed be sundrie Acts of Parliaments, and of lawful General Assemblies.

THE PREFACE

The Estaitis of *Scotland* with the Inhabitants of the same professand *Christ Jesus* his haly Evangel, to their natural Countrymen, and unto all uther realmes professand the same Lord *Jesus* with them, wish Grace, Mercie and Peace fra God the Father of our Lord *Jesus Christ*, with the Spirit of richteous Judgement, for Salvatioun.

Lang have we thristed, dear Brethren, to have notified to the Warld the Sum of that Doctrine quhilk we professe, and for the quhilk we have susteined Infamie and Danger: Bot sik hes bene the Rage of Sathan againis us, and againis *Christ Jesus* his eternal Veritie latlie now againe born amangst us, that to this daie na Time hes been graunted unto us to cleir our Consciences, as maist gladlie we wald have done. For how we have been tossit heirtofoir, the maist part of *Europe*, as we suppose, dois understand.

But seing that of the infinit Gudnes of our God (quha never sufferis his afflickit utterlie to be confoundit) abone Expectation we have obteined sum Rest and Libertie, we culd not bot set furth this brefe and plaine Confessioun of sik Doctrine as is proponed unto us, and as we beleeve and professe; partlie for Satisfactioun of our Brethren quhais hartis, we nathing doubt, have been and ʒit ar woundit be the despichtful rayling of sik as ʒit have not learned to speke well: And partlie for stapping the mouthis of impudent blasphemers, quha bauldlie damne that quhilk they have nouther heard nor ʒit understude.

Not that we judge that the cankred malice of sik is abill to be cured be this our simple confession; na, we knaw that the sweet savoure of the evangel is and sal be deathe unto the sonnes of perditioun. Bot we have chief respect to our weak and infirme brethren, to quham we wald communicate the bottom of our hartes, leist that they be troubiled or carried awaie be diversity of rumoris, quhilk Sathan spredis againist us to the defeating of this our maist godlie interprize: Protestand that gif onie man will note in this our confessioun onie Artickle or sentence repugnand to Gods halie word, that it wald pleis him of his gentleness and for christian charities sake to admonish us of the same in writing; and we upon our honoures and fidelitie, be Gods grace do promise unto him satisfactioun fra the mouth of God, that is, fra his haly scriptures, or else reformation of that quhilk he sal prove to be amisse. For God we take to recorde in our consciences, that fra our heartis we abhorre all sectis of heresie and all teachers of erronious doctrine: and that with all humilitie we imbrace the purity of *Christs* Gospell, quhilk is the onelie fude of our sauls, and therefoir sa precious unto us, that we ar determined to suffer the extremest of warldlie daunger, rather than that we will suffer our selves to be defraudit of the sam. For heirof we ar maist certainlie perswadit, that quhasumever denieis Christ Jesus, or is aschamit of him in the presence of men, sal be denyit befoir the Father, and befoir his haly Angels. And therefoir be the assistance of the michtie Spirit of the same our Lord Jesus Christ, we firmelie purpose to abide to the end in the confessioun of this our faith, as be Artickles followis.

ARTICLE I

OF GOD

We confesse and acknawledge ane onelie God, to whom only we must cleave, whom onelie we must serve, whom onelie we must worship, and in whom onelie we must put our trust. Who is Eternall, Infinit, Unmeasurable, Incomprehensible, Omnipotent, Invisible: ane in substance, and 3it distinct in thre personnis, the Father, the Sone, and the holie Gost. Be whom we confesse and beleve all thingis in hevin and eirth aswel Visible as Invisible, to have been created, to be reteined in their being, and to be ruled and guyded be his inscrutable Providence, to sik end, as his Eternall Wisdome, Gudnes, and Justice hes appoynted them, to the manifestatioun of his awin glorie.

ARTICLE II

OF THE CREATIOUN OF MAN

We confesse and acknawledge this our GOD to have created man, to wit, our first father *Adam*, to his awin image and similitude, to whome he gave wisdome, lordship, justice, free-wil, and cleir knawledge of himselfe, sa that in the haill nature of man there culd be noted no imperfectioun. Fra quhilk honour and perfectioun, man and woman did bothe fal: the woman being deceived be the Serpent, and man obeying the voyce of the woman, both conspyring against the Soveraigne Majestie of GOD, who in expressed words had before threatned deith, gif they presumed to eit of the forbidden tre.

ARTICLE III

OF ORIGINAL SINNE

Be quhilk transgressioun, commonlie called Original sinne, wes the Image of GOD utterlie defaced in man, and he and his posteritie of nature become enimies to GOD, slaves to Sathan, and servandis unto sin. In samekle that deith everlasting hes had, and sall have power and dominioun over all that have not been, ar not, or sal not be regenerate from above: quhilk regeneratioun is wrocht be the power of the holie Gost, working in the hartes of the elect of GOD, ane assured faith in the promise of GOD, reveiled to us in his word, be quhilk faith we apprehend Christ Jesus, with the graces and benefites promised in him.

ARTICLE IV

OF THE REVELATIOUN OF THE PROMISE

For this we constantlie beleeve, that GOD, after the feirfull and horrible defectioun of man fra his obedience, did seek *Adam* againe, call upon him, rebuke his sinne, convict him of the same, and in the end made unto him ane most joyful promise, to wit, *That the seed of the woman suld break down the serpents head*, that is, he suld destroy the works of the Devill. Quhilk promise, as it was repeated, and made mair cleare from time to time; so was it imbraced with joy, and maist constantlie received of al the faithfull, from *Adam* to *Noe*, from *Noe* to *Abraham*, from *Abraham* to *David*, and so furth to the incarnatioun of *Christ Jesus*, all (we meane the faithfull Fathers under the Law) did see the joyfull daie of *Christ Jesus*, and did rejoyce.

ARTICLE V

OF THE CONTINUANCE, INCREASE, AND PRESERVATIOUN OF THE KIRK

We maist constantly beleeve, that God preserved, instructed, multiplied, honoured, decored, and from death called to life, his Kirk in all ages fra *Adam*, till the cumming of *Christ Jesus* in the flesh. For *Abraham* he called from his Fathers cuntry, him he instructed, his seede he multiplied; the same he marveilouslie preserved, and mair marveilouslie delivered from the bondage and tyrannie of *Pharaoh*; to them he gave his lawes, constitutions and ceremonies; them he possessed in the land of *Canaan*; to them after Judges, and after *Saul*, he gave *David* to be king, to whome hee made promise, that of the fruite of his loynes suld ane sit for ever upon his regall seat. To this same people from time to time he sent prophets, to reduce them to the right way of their God: from the quhilk oftentimes they declined be idolatry. And albeit that for their stubborne contempt of Justice, he was compelled to give them in the hands of their enimies, as befoir was threatned be the mouth of *Moses*, in sa meikle that the haly cittie was destroyed, the temple burnt with fire, and the haill land left desolate the space of lxx years: ȝit of mercy did he reduce them againe to *Jerusalem*, where the cittie and temple were reedified, and they against all temptations and assaultes of Sathan did abide, till the *Messias* come, according to the promise.

Article VI

OF THE INCARNATION OF CHRIST JESUS

Quhen the fulnes of time came, God sent his Sonne, his eternall Wisdome, the substance of his awin glory in this warld, quha tuke the nature of man-head of the substance of woman, to wit, of a virgine, and that be operatioun of the holie Ghost: and so was borne the just seede of *David*, the Angell of the great counsell of God, the very *Messias* promised, whome we confesse and acknawledge *Emmanuel*, very God and very man, two perfit natures united, and joyned in one persoun. Be quhilk our Confessioun we condemne the damnable and pestilent heresies of *Arius, Marcion, Eutyches, Nestorius*, and sik uthers, as either did denie the eternitie of his God-head, or the veritie of his humaine nature, or confounded them, or ȝit devided them.

Article VII

WHY IT BEHOOVED THE MEDIATOR TO
BE VERY GOD AND VERY MAN

We acknawledge and confesse, that this maist wonderous conjunction betwixt the God-head and the man-head in *Christ Jesus*, did proceed from the eternall and immutable decree of God, from quhilk al our salvatioun springs and depends.

Article VIII

OF ELECTION

For that same eternall God and Father, who of meere grace elected us in *Christ Jesus* his Sonne, befoir the foundatioun of the warld was laide, appointed him to be our Head, our Brother, our Pastor, and great Bischop of our sauls. Bot because that the enimitie betwixt the justice of God and our sins was sik, that na flesh be it selfe culd or might have attained unto God: It behooved that the Sonne of God suld descend unto us, and tak himselfe a bodie of our bodie, flesh of our flesh, and bone of our bones, and so become the Mediator betwixt God and man, giving power to so many as beleeve in him, to be the sonnes of God; as himselfe dois witnesse, *I passe up to my Father, and unto ʒour Father, to my God, and unto ʒour God.* Be quhilk maist holie fraternitie, quhatsaever wee have tynt in *Adam*, is restored unto us agayne. And for this cause, ar we not affrayed to cal God our Father, not sa meikle because he hes created us, quhilk we have common with the reprobate; as for that, that he hes given to us his onely Sonne, to be our brother, and given to us grace, to acknawledge and imbrace him for our onlie Mediatour, as before is said. It behooved farther the Messias and Redemer to be very God and very man, because he was to underlie the punischment due for our transgressiouns, and to present himselfe in the presence of his Fathers Judgment, as in our persone, to suffer for our transgression and inobedience, be death to overcome him that was author of death. Bot because the onely God-head culd not suffer death, neither ʒit culd the onlie man-head overcome the samin, he joyned both togither in one persone, that the imbecillitie of the ane, suld suffer and be subject to death, quhilk we had deserved: And the infinit and invincible power of the uther, to wit, of the God-head, suld triumph and purchesse to us life, libertie, and perpetuall victory: And so we confes, and maist undoubtedly beleeve.

ARTICLE IX

OF CHRIST'S DEATH, PASSION, AND BURIAL

That our Lord *Jesus* offered himselfe a voluntary Sacrifice unto his Father for us, that he suffered contradiction of sinners, that he was wounded and plagued for our transgressiouns, that hee being the cleane innocent Lambe of God, was damned in the presence of an earthlie judge, that we suld be absolved befoir the tribunal seat of our God. That hee suffered not onlie the cruell death of the Crosse, quhilk was accursed be the sentence of God; bot also that he suffered for a season the wrath of his Father, quhilk sinners had deserved. Bot ȝit we avow that he remained the only welbeloved and blessed Sonne of his Father, even in the middest of his anguish and torment, quhilk hee suffered in bodie and saule, to mak the full satisfaction for the sinnes of the people. After the quhilk we confesse and avow, that there remaines na uther Sacrifice for sinne, quhilk gif ony affirme, we nathing dout to avow that they ar blasphemous against *Christs* death, and the everlasting purgatioun and satisfactioun purchased to us be the same.

ARTICLE X

OF THE RESURRECTION

We undoubtedlie beleeve, that in sa mekle as it wes impossible, that the dolours of death sulde reteine in bondage the Author of life, that our LORD JESUS crucified, dead and buryed, quha descended into hell, did ryse agayne for our Justificatioun, and destroying of him quha wes the Author of death, brocht life againe to us, that wer subject to death, and to the bondage of the same. We knaw that his Resurrectioun wes confirmed be the testimonie of his verie Enemies, be the resurrectioun of the dead, quhais Sepultures did oppen, and they did ryse, and appeared to mony, within the Cittie of *Jerusalem*. It wes also confirmed be the testimonie of his Angels, and be the senses and judgements of his Apostles, and of uthers, quha had conversatioun, and did eate and drink with him, after his Resurrection.

Article XI

OF THE ASCENSION

We nathing doubt, bot the self same bodie, quhilk was borne of the Virgine, was crucified, dead, and buried, and quhilk did rise againe, did ascend into the heavens, for the accomplishment of all thinges: Quhere in our names, and for our comfort, he hes received all power in heaven and eirth, quhere he sittes at the richt hand of the Father, inaugurate in his kingdome, Advocate and onlie Mediator for us. Quhilk glorie, honour, and prerogative, he alone amonges the brethren sal possess, till that all his Enimies be made his futestule, as that we undoubtedlie beleeve they sall be in the finall Judgment: To the Execution whereof we certainelie beleve, that the same our Lord JESUS sall visiblie returne, as that hee was sene to ascend. And then we firmely beleve, that the time of refreshing and restitutioun of all things sall cum, in samekle that thir, that fra the beginning have suffered violence, injurie, and wrang, for richteousnes sake, sal inherit that blessed immortalitie promised fra the beginning.

Bot contrariwise the stubburne, inobedient, cruell oppressours, filthie personis, idolaters, and all such sortes of unfaithfull, sal be cast in the dungeoun of utter darkenesse, where their worme sall not die, nether 3it their fyre sall bee extinguished. The remembrance of quhilk day, and of the Judgement to be executed in the same, is not onelie to us ane brydle, whereby our carnal lustes are refrained, bot alswa sik inestimable comfort, that nether may the threatning of worldly Princes, nether 3it the feare of temporal death and present danger, move us to renounce and forsake that blessed societie, quhilk we the members have with our Head and onelie Mediator CHRIST JESUS: Whom we confesse and avow to be the Messias promised, the onlie Head of his Kirk, our just Lawgiver, our onlie hie Priest, Advocate, and Mediator. In quhilk honoures and offices, gif man or Angell presume to intruse themself, we utterlie detest and abhorre them, as blasphemous to our Soveraigne and supreme Governour CHRIST JESUS.

Article XII

OF FAITH IN THE HOLY GOSTE

This our Faith and the assurance of the same, proceeds not fra flesh and blude, that is to say, fra na natural poweris within us, bot is the inspiration of the holy Gost: Whome we confesse GOD equall with the Father and with his Sonne, quha sanctifyis us, and bringis us in al veritie be his awin operation, without whome we sulde remaine for ever enimies to God, and ignorant of his Sonne *Christ Jesus*; for of nature we are so dead, so blind, and so perverse, that nether can we feill when we are pricked, see the licht when it shines, nor assent to the will of God when it is reveiled, unles the Spirit of the Lord *Jesus* quicken that quhilk is dead, remove the darknesse from our myndes, and bowe our stubburne hearts to the obedience of his blessed will. And so as we confesse, that God the Father created us, when we were not, as his Sonne our Lord *Jesus* redeemed us, when wee were enimies to him; so also do we confesse that the holy Gost doth sanctifie and regenerat us, without all respect of ony merite proceeding from us, be it before, or be it after our Regeneration. To speak this ane thing 3it in mair plaine words: As we willingly spoyle our selves of all honour and gloir of our awin Creation and Redemption, so do we also of our Regeneration and Sanctification, for of our selves we ar not sufficient to think one gude thocht, bot he quha hes begun the wark in us, is onlie he that continewis us in the same, to the praise and glorie of his undeserved grace.

Article XIII

OF THE CAUSE OF GUDE WARKIS

Sa that the cause of gude warkis, we confesse to be not our free wil, bot the Spirit of the Lord *Jesus*, who dwelling in our hearts be trewe faith, bringis furth sik warkis, as God hes prepared for us to walke in. For this wee maist boldelie affirme, that blasphemy it is to say, that *Christ* abydes in the heartes of sik, as in whome there is no spirite of sanctification. And therefore we feir not to affirme, that murtherers, oppressers, cruell persecuters, adulterers, huremongers, filthy persouns, Idolaters, drunkards, thieves, and al workers of iniquity, have nether trew faith, nether ony portion of the Spirit of the Lord JESUS, so long as obstinatlie they continew in their wickednes. For how soone that ever the Spirit of the Lord JESUS, quhilk Gods elect children receive be trew faith, taks possession in the heart of ony man, so soone dois he regenerate and renew the same man. So that he beginnis to hait that quhilk before he loved, and begins to love that quhilk befoir he hated; and fra thine cummis that continuall battell, quhilk is betwixt the flesh and the Spirit in Gods children, till the flesh and natural man, according to the awin corruption, lustes for things pleisand and delectable unto the self, and grudges in adversity, is lyfted up in prosperity, and at every moment is prone and reddie to offend the majestie of God. Bot the spirite of God, quhilk gives witnessing to our spirite, that we are the sonnes of God, makis us to resist filthie plesures, and to groane in Gods presence, for deliverance fra this bondage of corruption; and finally to triumph over sin, that it reygne not in our mortal bodyis. This battell hes not the carnal men, being destitute of Gods Spirite, bot dois followe and obey sinne with greedines, and without repentance, even as the Devill, and their corrupt lustes do prick them. Bot the sonnes of God, as before wes said, dois fecht against sinne; dois sob and murne, when they perceive themselves tempted in iniquitie; and gif they fal, they rise againe with earnest and unfained repentance: And thir thingis they do not be their awin power, bot be the power of the Lord *Jesus*, without whom they were able to do nothing.

ARTICLE XIV

WHAT WARKIS ARE REPUTIT GUDE BEFOIR GOD

We confesse and acknawledge, that God hes given to man his holy Law, in quhilk not only ar forbidden all sik warkes as displeis and offend his godly Majestie, but alswa ar commanded al sik as pleis him, and as hes promised to rewaird. And thir warkes be of twa sortes. The ane are done to the honour of God, the uther to the profite of our

Nichtbouris; and both have the reveiled will of God for their
assurance. To have ane God, to worschip and honour him, to
call upon him in all our troubles, reverence his holy name, to
heare his word, to beleve the same, to communicate with his
holy Sacraments, are the warkes of the first Tabill. To honour
Father, Mother, Princes, Rulers, and superiour powers; to
love them, to support them, ȝea to obey their charges (not
repugning to the commaundment of God), to save the lives
of innocents, to represse tyrannie, to defend the oppressed,
to keepe our bodies cleane and halie, to live in sobernes and
temperance, to deall justlie with all men both in word and
deed; and finally, to represse all appetite of our Nichbouris
hurt, are the gude warkes of the secund Tabill, quhilk are
maist pleising and acceptabill unto God, as thir warkes that
are commanded be himselfe. The contrary quhairof is sinne
maist odious, quhilk alwayes displeisis him, and provokes
him to anger: As not to call upon him alone, when we have
need; not to hear his word with reverence, to contemne
and despise it; to have or worschip idols, to maintene and
defend Idolatrie; lichtlie to esteeme the reverend name of
God; to prophane, abuse, or contemne the Sacraments of
Christ Jesus; to disobey or resist ony that God hes placed
in authoritie (quhil they passe not over the bounds of their
office); to murther, or to consent thereto, to beare hatred,
or to let innocent blude bee sched, gif wee may withstand it.
And finally, the transgression of ony uther commandement
in the first or secund Tabill, we confesse and affirme to be
sinne, by the quhilk Gods anger and displesure is kindled
against the proud unthankfull warld. So that gude warkes
we affirme to be thir onlie, that are done in faith, and at God
commandment, quha in his Lawe hes expressed what the
thingis be that pleis him. And evill warkis we affirme not only
thir that expressedly ar done against Gods commaundement:
bot thir alswa that in matteris of Religioun, and worschipping
of God, hes na uther assurance bot the inventioun and
opinioun of man: quhilk God fra the beginning hes ever
rejected, as be the Prophet *Esay*, and be our Maister CHRIST
JESUS we ar taught in thir words, *In vaine do they worschip
me, teaching the doctrines the precepts of men.*

ARTICLE XV

OF THE PERFECTIOUN OF THE LAW,
AND THE IMPERFECTIOUN OF MAN

The Law of God we confesse and acknawledge maist just, maist equall, maist halie, and maist perfite, commaunding thir thingis, quhilk being wrocht in perfectioun, were abill to give life, and abill to bring man to eternall felicitie. Bot our nature is sa corrupt, sa weake, and sa unperfite, that we ar never abill to fulfill the warkes of the Law in perfectioun. Зеа, gif we say we have na sinne, evin after we are regenerate, we deceive our selves, and the veritie of God is not in us. And therefore, it behovis us to apprehend *Christ Jesus* with his justice and satisfaction, quha is the end and accomplishment of the Law, be quhome we ar set at this liberty, that the curse and malediction of God fall not upon us, albeit we fulfill not the same in al pointes. For God the Father beholding us, in the body of his Sonne *Christ Jesus*, acceptis our imperfite obedience, as it were perfite, and covers our warks, quhilk ar defyled with mony spots, with the justice of his Sonne. We do not meane that we ar so set at liberty, that we awe na obedience to the Law (for that before wee have plainly confessed), bot this we affirme, that na man in eird (*Christ Jesus* onlie except) hes given, gives, or sall give in worke, that obedience to the Law, quhilk the Law requiris. Bot when we have done all things, we must falle down and unfeinedly confesse, that we are unprofitable servands. And therefore, quhosoever boastis themselves of the merits of their awin works, or put their trust in the works of Supererogation, boast themselves in that quhilk is nocht, and put their trust in damnable Idolatry.

ARTICLE XVI

OF THE KIRK

As we beleve in ane God, Father, Sonne, and haly Ghaist; sa do we maist constantly beleeve, that from the beginning there hes bene, and now is, and to the end of the warld sall be, ane Kirk, that is to say, ane company and multitude of men chosen of God, who richtly worship and imbrace him be trew faith in *Christ Jesus*, quha is the only head of the same Kirk, quhilk alswa is the bodie and spouse of *Christ Jesus*, quhilk Kirk is catholike, that is, universal, because it conteinis the Elect of all ages, of all realmes, nations, and tongues, be they of the *Jewes*, or be they of the Gentiles, quha have communion and societie with God the Father, and with his Son *Christ Jesus*, throw the sanctification of his haly Spirit: and therefore it is called the communioun, not of prophane persounes, bot of Saincts, quha as citizenis of the heavenly *Jerusalem*, have the fruitioun of the maist inestimable benefites, to wit, of ane God, ane Lord *Jesus*, ane faith, and ane baptisme: Out of the quhilk Kirk, there is nouther lyfe, nor eternall felicitie. And therefore we utterly abhorre the blasphemie of them that affirme, that men quhilk live according to equitie and justice, sal be saved, quhat Religioun that ever they have professed. For as without *Christ Jesus* there is nouther life nor salvation; so sal there nane be participant therof, bot sik as the Father hes given unto his Sonne *Christ Jesus*, and they that in time cum unto him, avowe his doctrine, and beleeve into him, we comprehend the children with the faithfull parentes. This Kirk is invisible, knawen onelie to God, quha alane knawis whome he hes chosen; and comprehends as weill (as said is) the Elect that be departed, commonlie called the *Kirk Triumphant*, and they that ʒit live and fecht against sinne and *Sathan* as sall live hereafter.

ARTICLE XVII

OF THE IMMORTALITIE OF THE SAULES

The Elect departed are in peace and rest fra their labours: Not that they sleep, and come to a certaine oblivion, as some Phantastickes do affirme; bot that they are delivered fra all feare and torment, and all temptatioun, to quhilk we and all Goddis Elect are subject in this life, and therefore do beare the name of the *Kirk Militant*: As contrariwise, the reprobate and unfaithfull departed have anguish, torment, and paine, that cannot be expressed. Sa that nouther are the ane nor the uther in sik sleepe that they feele not joy or torment, as the Parable of *Christ Jesus* in the 16th of *Luke,* his words to the thiefe, and thir wordes of the saules crying under the Altar, *O Lord, thou that art righteous and just, How lang sall thou not revenge our blude upon thir that dwellis in the Eird?* dois testifie.

ARTICLE XVIII

OF THE NOTIS, BE THE QUHILK THE TREWE KIRK IS DECERNIT FRA THE FALSE, AND QUHA SALL BE JUDGE OF THE DOCTRINE

Because that *Sathan* from the beginning hes laboured to deck his pestilent Synagoge with the title of the Kirk of God, and hes inflamed the hertes of cruell murtherers to persecute, trouble, and molest the trewe Kirk and members thereof, as *Cain* did *Abell, Ismael Isaac, Esau Jacob,* and the haill Priesthood of the *Jewes Christ Jesus* himselfe, and his Apostles after him. It is ane thing maist requisite, that the true Kirk be decerned fra the filthie Synagogues, be cleare and perfite notes, least we being deceived, receive and imbrace, to our awin condemnation, the ane for the uther. The notes, signes, and assured takens whereby the immaculate Spouse of *Christ Jesus* is knawen fra the horrible harlot, the Kirk malignant, we affirme, are nouther Antiquitie, Title usurpit, lineal Descence, Place appointed, nor multitude of men approving ane error. For *Cain,* in age and title, was preferred to *Abel* and *Seth: Jerusalem* had prerogative above all places of the eird, where alswa were the Priests lineally descended fra *Aaron,* and greater number followed the Scribes, Pharisies, and Priestes, then unfainedly beleeved and approved *Christ Jesus* and his doctrine: And 3it, as we suppose, no man of sound judgment will grant, that ony of the forenamed were the Kirk of God. The notes therefore of the trew Kirk of God we beleeve, confesse, and avow to be, first, the trew preaching of the Worde of God, into the quhilk God hes revealed himselfe unto us, as the writings of the Prophets and Apostles dois declair. Secundly, the right administration of the Sacraments of *Christ Jesus,* quhilk man be annexed unto the word and promise of

God, to seale and confirme the same in our hearts. Last, Ecclesiastical discipline uprightlie ministred, as Goddis Worde prescribes, whereby vice is repressed, and vertew nurished. Wheresoever then thir former notes are seene, and of ony time continue (be the number never so fewe, about two or three), there, without all doubt, is the trew Kirk of *Christ*: Who, according unto his promise, is in the middis of them. Not that universall, of quhilk we have before spoken, bot particular, sik as wes in *Corinthus*, *Galatia*, *Ephesus*, and uther places, in quhilk the ministrie wes planted be *Paull*, and were of himselfe named the kirks of God. And sik kirks, we the inhabitantis of the Realme of *Scotland*, professoris of *Christ Jesus*, professis our selfis to have in our citties, townes, and places reformed, for the doctrine taucht in our Kirkis, conteined in the writen Worde of God, to wit, in the buiks of the Auld and New Testamentis, in those buikis we meane quhilk of the ancient have been reputed canonicall. In the quhilk we affirme, that all thingis necessary to be beleeved for the salvation of mankinde is sufficiently expressed. The interpretation quhairof, we confesse, neither appertaines to private nor publick persone, nether 3it to ony Kirk, for ony preheminence or prerogative, personallie or locallie, quhilk ane hes above ane uther, bot apperteines to the Spirite of God, be the quhilk also the Scripture was written. When controversie then happines, for the right understanding of ony place or sentence of Scripture, or for the reformation of ony abuse within the Kirk of God, we ought not sa meikle to luke what men before us have said or done, as unto that quhilk the halie Ghaist uniformelie speakes within the body of the Scriptures, and unto that quhilk *Christ Jesus* himselfe did, and commanded to be done. For this is ane thing universallie granted, that the Spirite of God, quhilk is the Spirite of unitie, is in nathing contrarious unto himselfe. Gif then the interpretation, determination, or sentence of ony Doctor, Kirk, or Councell, repugne to the plaine Worde of God, written in ony uther place of the Scripture, it is a thing maist certaine, that there is not the true understanding and meaning of the haly Ghaist, although that Councels, Realmes, and Nations have approved and received the same. For we dare non receive or admit ony interpretation quhilk repugnes to ony principall point of our faith, or to ony uther plaine text of Scripture, or ʒit unto the rule of charitie.

Article XIX

OF THE AUTHORITIE OF THE SCRIPTURES

As we beleeve and confesse the Scriptures of God sufficient to instruct and make the man of God perfite, so do we affirme and avow the authoritie of the same to be of God, and nether to depend on men nor angelis. We affirme, therefore, that sik as allege the Scripture to have na uther authoritie bot that quhilk it hes received from the Kirk, to be blasphemous against God, and injurious to the trew Kirk, quhilk alwaies heares and obeyis the voice of her awin Spouse and Pastor; bot takis not upon her to be maistres over the samin.

Article XX

OF GENERALL COUNCELLIS, OF THEIR POWER,
AUTHORITIE, AND CAUSE OF THEIR CONVENTION

As we do not rashlie damne that quhilk godly men, assembled togither in generall Councel lawfully gathered, have proponed unto us; so without just examination dare we not receive quhatsoever is obtruded unto men under the name of generall Councelis: For plaine it is, as they wer men, so have some of them manifestlie erred, and that in matters of great weight and importance. So farre then as the councell previs the determination and commandement that it gives bee the plaine Worde of God, so soone do we reverence and imbrace the same. Bot gif men, under the name of a councel, pretend to forge unto us new artickles of our faith, or to make constitutionis repugning to the Word of God; then utterlie we must refuse the same as the doctrine of Devils, quhilk drawis our saules from the voyce of our onlie God to follow the doctrines and constitutiones of men. The cause then quhy that generall Councellis convened, was nether to make ony perpetual Law, quhilk God before had not maid, nether ʒit to forge new Artickles of our beleife, nor to give the Word of God authoritie; meikle les to make that to be his Word, or ȝit the trew interpretation of the same, quhilk wes not before be his haly will expressed in his Word: Bot the cause of Councellis (we meane of sik as merite the name of Councellis) wes partlie for confutation of heresies, and for giving publick confession of their faith to the posteritie of Goddis written Word, and not by ony opinion or prerogative that they culd not erre, be reasson of their generall assemblie: And this we judge to have bene the chiefe cause of general Councellis. The uther wes for gude policie, and ordour to be constitute and observed in the Kirk, quhilk, as in the house of God, is becummis *al things to be done decently and in ordour*. Not that we think that any policie and an ordour in ceremonies can be appoynted for al ages, times, and places: For as ceremonies, sik as men have devised, ar bot temporall; so may and aucht they to be changed, when they rather foster superstition then that they edifie the Kirk using the same.

Article XXI

OF THE SACRAMENTIS

As the Fatheris under the Law, besides the veritie of the Sacrifices, had twa chiefe Sacramentes, to wit, Circumcision and the Passeover, the despisers and contemners whereof were not reputed for Gods people; sa do we acknawledge and confesse that we now in the time of the Evangell have twa chiefe Sacramentes, onelie instituted be the Lord *Jesus*, and commanded to be used of all they that will be reputed members of his body, to wit, Baptisme and the Supper or Table of the Lord *Jesus*, called the Communion of his Body and his Blude. And thir Sacramentes, as weil of Auld as of New Testament, now instituted of God, not onelie to make ane visible difference betwixt his people and they that wes without his league: Bot also to exerce the faith of his Children, and, be participation of the same Sacramentes, to seill in their hearts the assurance of his promise, and of that most blessed conjunction, union and societie, quhilk the elect have with their head *Christ Jesus*. And this we utterlie damne the vanitie of thay that affirme Sacramentes to be nathing ellis bot naked and baire signes. No, wee assuredlie beleeve that be Baptisme we ar ingrafted in *Christ Jesus*, to be made partakers of his justice, be quhilk our sinnes ar covered and remitted. And alswa, that in the Supper richtlie used, *Christ Jesus* is so joined with us, that hee becummis very nurishment and fude of our saules. Not that we imagine anie transubstantiation of bread into *Christes* body, and of wine into his naturall blude, as the *Papistes* have perniciouslie taucht and damnablie beleeved; bot this unioun and conjunction, quhilk we have with the body and blude of *Christ Jesus* in the richt use of the Sacraments, wrocht be operatioun of the haly Ghaist, who by trew faith carryis us above al things that are visible, carnal, and earthly, and makes us to feede upon the body and blude of *Christ Jesus*, quhilk wes anes broken and shed for us, quhilk now is in heaven, and appearis in the presence of his Father for us: And 3it notwithstanding the far distance of place quhilk is betwixt his body now glorified in heaven and us now mortal in this eird, 3it we man assuredly beleve that the bread quhilk wee break, is the communion of *Christes* bodie, and the cupe quhilk we blesse, is the communion of his blude. So that we confesse, and undoubtedlie beleeve, that the faithfull, in the richt use of the Lords Table, do so eat the bodie and drinke the blude of the Lord *Jesus*, that he remaines in them, and they in him: 3ea, they are maid flesh of his flesh, and bone of his bones; that as the eternall God-head hes given to the flesh of *Christ Jesus* (quhilk of the awin conditioun and nature wes mortal and corruptible) life and immortalitie; so dois *Christ Jesus* his flesh and blude eattin and drunkin be us, give unto us the same prerogatives. Quhilk, albeit we confesse are nether given unto us at that time onelie, nether 3it be the proper power and vertue of the Sacrament onelie; 3it we affirme that the faithfull, in the richt use of the Lords Table, hes conjunction with *Christ Jesus*, as the naturall man can not apprehend: 3ea, and farther we affirme, that albeit the faithfull, oppressed be negligence and manlie infirmitie, dois not profite sameikle as they wald, in the verie instant action of the Supper; 3it sall it after bring frute furth, as livelie seid sawin in gude ground. For the haly Spirite, quhilk can never be divided fra the richt institution of the Lord *Jesus*, wil not frustrat the faithfull of the fruit of that mysticall action: Bot all thir, we say, cummis of trew faith, quhilk apprehendis *Christ Jesus*, who only makis this Sacrament effectuall unto us. And therefore, whosoever sclanders us, as that we affirme or beleeve Sacraments to be naked and bair Signes, do injurie unto us, and speaks against the manifest trueth. Bot this liberallie and franklie we confesse, that we make ane distinctioun betwixt *Christ Jesus* in his eternall substance, and betwixt the Elements of the Sacramentall Signes. So that wee will nether worship the Signes, in place of that quhilk is signified be them, nether ʒit doe we despise, and interpret them as unprofitable and vaine, bot do use them with all reverence, examining our selves diligentlie before that so we do; because we are assured be the mouth of the Apostle, *That sik as eat of that bread, and drink of that coup unworthelie, are guiltie of the bodie and blude of* Christ Jesus.

Article XXII

OF THE RICHT ADMINISTRATIOUN OF THE SACRAMENTIS

That Sacramentis be richtlie ministrat, we judge twa things requisite: The ane, that they be ministrat be lauchful Ministers, whom we affirme to be only they that ar appoynted to the preaching of the word, into quhais mouthes God hes put sum Sermon of exhortation, they being men lauchfullie chosen thereto be sum Kirk. The uther, that they be ministrat in sik elements, and in sik sort, as God hes appointed; else, we affirme, that they cease to be the richt Sacraments of *Christ Jesus*. And therefore it is that we flee the doctrine of the *Papistical* Kirk, in participatioun of their sacraments; first, because their Ministers are na Ministers of *Christ Jesus*; ʒea (quhilk is mair horrible) they suffer wemen, whome the haly Ghaist will not suffer to teache in the Congregatioun, to baptize: And secundly, because they have so adulterate both the one Sacrament and the uther with their awin inventions, that no part of *Christs* action abydes in the originall puritie: For Oyle, Salt, Spittill, and sik lyke in Baptisme, ar bot mennis inventiounis. Adoration,

Veneration, bearing throw streitis and townes, and keiping of bread in boxis or buistis, ar prophanatioun of *Christs* Sacramentis, and na use of the same: For *Christ Jesus* saide, *Take, eat,* &c., *do ʒe this in remembrance of me.* Be quhilk words and charge he sanctifyed bread and wine, to the Sacrament of his halie bodie and blude, to the end that the ane suld be eaten, and that all suld drinke of the uther, and not that thay suld be keiped to be worshipped and honoured as God, as the *Papistes* have done heirtofore. Who also committed Sacrilege, steilling from the people the ane parte of the Sacrament, to wit, the blessed coupe. Moreover, that the Sacramentis be richtly used, it is required, that the end and cause why the Sacramentis were institute, be understanded and observed, asweil of the minister as of the receiveris: For gif the opinion be changed in the receiver, the richt use ceassis; quhilk is maist evident be the rejection of the sacrifices: As also gif the teacher planely teache fals doctrine, quhilk were odious and abhominable before God (albeit they were his awin ordinance) because that wicked men use them to an uther end than God hes ordaned. The same affirme we of the Sacraments in the *Papistical* kirk; in quhilk, we affirme, the haill action of the Lord *Jesus* to be adulterated, asweill in the external forme, as in the end and opinion. Quhat *Christ Jesus* did, and commanded to be done, is evident be the Evangelistes and be Saint *Paull:* quhat the Preist dois at his altar we neid not to rehearse. The end and cause of Christs institution, and why the selfsame suld be used, is expressed in thir words, *Doe ʒe this in remembrance of me, als oft as ʒe sall eit of this bread, and drinke of this coupe, ʒe sall shaw furth,* that is, extoll, preach, magnifie and praise *the Lords death, till he cum.* Bot to quhat end, and in what opinioun the Preists say their Messe, let the wordes of the same, their awin Doctouris and wrytings witnes: To wit, that they, as Mediatoris betwix *Christ* and his Kirk, do offer unto God the Father, a Sacrifice propitiatorie for the sinnes of the quick and the dead. Quhilk doctrine, as blasphemous to *Christ Jesus,* and making derogation to the sufficiencie of his only Sacrifice, once offered for purgatioun of all they that sall be sanctifyed, we utterly abhorre, detest and renounce.

Article XXIII

TO WHOME SACRAMENTIS APPERTEINE

We confesse & acknawledge that Baptisme apperteinis asweil to the infants of the faithfull, as unto them that be of age and discretion: And so we damne the error of the *Anabaptists*, who denies baptisme to apperteine to Children, before that they have faith and understanding. Bot the Supper of the Lord, we confesse to appertaine to sik onely as be of the houshald of Faith, and can trie and examine themselves, asweil in their faith, as in their dewtie towards their Nichtbouris; sik as eite and drink at that haly Table without faith, or being at dissension and division with their brethren, do eat unworthelie: And therefore it is, that in our Kirk our Ministers tak publick & particular examination, of the knawledge and conversation of sik as are to be admitted to the Table of the Lord *Jesus*.

Article XXIV

OF THE CIVILE MAGISTRATE

We confesse and acknawledge Empyres, Kingdomes, Dominiounis, and Citties to be distincted and ordained be God; the powers and authoritie in the same, be it of Emperours in their Empyres, of Kingis in their Realmes, Dukes and Princes in their Dominionis, and of utheris Magistrates in the Citties, to be Gods haly ordinance, ordained for manifestatioun of his awin glory, and for the singular profite and commoditie of mankind: So that whosoever goeth about to take away, or to confound the haill state of Civile policies, now long established; we affirme the same men not onely to be enimies to mankinde, but also wickedly to fecht against Goddis expressed will. Wee farther confesse and acknawledge, that sik persouns as are placed in authoritie ar to be loved, honoured, feared, and halden in most reverent estimatioun; because that they are the Lieu-tennents of God, in whose Sessiouns God himself dois sit and judge: 3ea, even the Judges & Princes themselves, to whome be God is given the sword, to the praise and defence of gude men, and to revenge and punish all open malefactors. Mairover, to Kings, Princes, Rulers and Magistrates, wee affirme that chieflie and most principallie the conservation and purgation of the Religioun apperteinis; so that not onlie they are appointed for Civill policie, bot also for maintenance of the trew Religioun, and for suppressing of Idolatrie and Superstitioun whatsoever: As in *David, Josaphat, Ezechias, Josias*, and utheris highlie commended for their zeale in that caise, may be espyed.

And therefore wee confesse and avow, that sik as resist the supreme power, doing that thing quhilk appertains to his charge, do resist Goddis ordinance; and therefore cannot be guiltles. And farther we affirme, that whosoever denies unto them ayde, their counsell and comfort, quhiles the Princes and Rulers vigilantly travell in execution of their office, that the same men deny their helpe, support and counsell to God, quha, be the presence of his Lieu-tennent, dois crave it of them.

Article XXV

OF THE GUIFTES FREELY GIVEN TO THE KIRK

Albeit that the Worde of God trewly preached, and the Sacraments richtlie ministred, and Discipline executed according to the Worde of God, be the certaine and infallible Signes of the trew Kirk, we meane not that everie particular persoun joyned with sik company, be ane elect member of *Christ Jesus*: For we acknawledge and confesse, that Dornell, Cockell, and Caffe may be sawen, grow, and in great aboundance lie in the middis of the Wheit, that is, the Reprobate may be joyned in the societie of the Elect, and may externally use with them the benefites of the worde and Sacraments: Bot sik being bot temporall professoures in mouth, but not in heart, do fall backe, and continew not to the end. And therefore have they na fruite of *Christs* death, Resurrection nor Ascension. Bot sik as with heart unfainedly beleeve, and with mouth bauldly confesse the Lord *Jesus*, as before we have said, sall most assuredly receive their guiftes: First, in this life, remission of sinnes, and that be only faith in *Christs* blude; in samekle, that albeit sinne remaine and continuallie abyde in thir our mortall bodies, ʒit it is not imputed unto us, bot is remitted, and covered with *Christs* Justice. Secundly, in the general Judgement, there sall be given to every man and woman resurrection of the flesh: For the Sea sall give her dead; the Earth, they that therein be inclosed; ʒea, the Eternall our God sall stretche out his hand on the dust, and the dead sall arise uncorruptible, and that in the substance of the selfe same flesh that every man now beiris, to receive according to their warkis, glory or punishment: For sik as now delyte in vanity, cruelty, filthynes, superstition or Idolatry, sal be adjudged to the fire unquencheable: In quhilk they sall be tormented for ever, asweill in their awin bodyes, as in their saules, quhilk now they give to serve the Devill in all abhomination. Bot sik as continew in weil doing to the end, bauldely professing the Lord *Jesus*, we constantly beleve, that they sall receive glorie, honor, and immortality, to reigne for ever in life everlasting with *Christ Jesus*, to whose glorified body all his Elect sall be made lyke, when he sall appeir againe in judgement, and sall rander up the kingdome to God his Father, who then sall bee, and ever sall remaine all in all things God blessed for ever: To whome, with the Sonne and with the haly Ghaist, be all honour and glorie, now and ever. *So be it.*

Arise (O Lord) and let thy enimies be confounded; let them flee from thy presence that hate thy godlie Name. Give thy servands strenth to speake thy word in bauldnesse, and let all Natiouns cleave to thy trew knawledge. Amen.

Thir Acts and Artickles ar red in the face of Parliament, and ratifyed be the thre Estatis, at Edinburgh the 17 day of August, the ʒeir of GOD 1560 ʒeiris.

No convenient edition of *The Scots Confession* has been in print for some time. This edition is a free translation, intended for the convenience of the average reader, and not of the scholar, who can make use of the original.

The Confession has twenty-five chapters, not arranged in the exact order of the Apostles' Creed, but everywhere consistent with it. These chapters vary considerably in length, partly because of relevance to matters then in dispute, and partly, perhaps, because of the writers to whom the first drafts had been assigned.

THE
CONFESSION
OF THE
Faith and Doctrine

Believed and professed by the

PROTESTANTS OF SCOTLAND

Exhibited to the Estates of Scotland in Parliament in August
1560 and approved by their public vote as doctrine founded
upon the infallible Word of God, and afterwards established
and publicly confirmed by various Acts of Parliament and of
lawful General Assemblies.

St Matthew 24:14
And this glad tidings of the Kingdom shall be preached
through the whole world for a witness to all nations; and
then shall the end come.

A MODERN TRANSLATION
by
James Bulloch

THE PREFACE

The Estates of Scotland, with the inhabitants of
Scotland who profess the holy Evangel of Jesus
Christ, to their fellow countrymen and to all other
nations who confess the Lord Jesus with them, wish
grace, mercy and peace from God the Father of
our Lord Jesus Christ, with the Spirit of righteous
judgment, for salvation.

Long have we thirsted, dear brethren, to have made
known to the world the doctrine which we profess
and for which we have suffered abuse and danger; but
such has been the rage of Satan against us, and against the
eternal truth of Christ now recently reborn among us, that
until this day we have had neither time nor opportunity to
set forth our faith, as gladly we would have done. For how
we have been afflicted until now the greater part of Europe,
we suppose, knows well.

But since by the infinite goodness of our God (who
never suffers His afflicted to be utterly confounded) we
have received unexpected rest and liberty, we could not
do other than set forth this brief and plain Confession of
that doctrine which is set before us, and which we believe
and confess; partly to satisfy our brethren whose hearts, we
suspect, have been and are grieved by the slanders against
us; and partly to silence impudent blasphemers who boldly
condemn that which they have not heard and do not
understand.

We do not suppose that such malice can be cured merely
by our Confession, for we know that the sweet savour of
the Gospel is, and shall be, death to the sons of perdition;
but we are considering chiefly our own weaker brethren, to
whom we would communicate our deepest thoughts, lest

they be troubled or carried away by the different rumours which Satan spreads against us to defeat our godly enterprise, protesting that if any man will note in our Confession any chapter or sentence contrary to God's Holy Word, that it would please him of his gentleness and for Christian charity's sake to inform us of it in writing; and we, upon our honour, do promise him that by God's grace we shall give him satisfaction from the mouth of God, that is, from Holy Scripture, or else we shall alter whatever he can prove to be wrong. For we call on God to record that from our hearts we abhor all heretical sects and all teachers of false doctrine, and that with all humility we embrace the purity of Christ's Gospel, which is the one food of our souls and therefore so precious to us that we are determined to suffer the greatest of worldly dangers, rather than let our souls be defrauded of it. For we are completely convinced that whoever denies Christ Jesus, or is ashamed of Him in the presence of men, shall be denied before the Father and before His holy angels. Therefore by the aid of the mighty Spirit of our Lord Jesus Christ we firmly intend to endure to the end in the confession of our faith, as in the following chapters.

CHAPTER I

GOD

We confess and acknowledge one God alone, to whom alone we must cleave, whom alone we must serve, whom only we must worship, and in whom alone we put our trust. Who is eternal, infinite, immeasurable, incomprehensible, omnipotent, invisible; one in substance and yet distinct in three persons, the Father, the Son and the Holy Ghost. By whom we confess and believe all things in heaven and earth, visible and invisible, to have been created, to be retained in their being, and to be ruled and guided by His inscrutable providence for such end as His eternal wisdom, goodness and justice have appointed, and to the manifestation of His own glory.

CHAPTER II

THE CREATION OF MAN

We confess and acknowledge that our God has created man, i.e., our first father, Adam, after His own image and likeness, to whom He gave wisdom, lordship, justice, free will and self-consciousness, so that in the whole nature of man no imperfection could be found. From this dignity and perfection man and woman both fell; the woman being deceived by the serpent and man obeying the voice of the woman, both conspiring against the sovereign majesty of God, who in clear words had previously threatened death if they presumed to eat of the forbidden tree.

CHAPTER III

ORIGINAL SIN

By this transgression, generally known as original sin, the image of God was utterly defaced in man, and he and his children became by nature hostile to God, slaves to Satan and servants to sin. And thus everlasting death has had, and shall have, power and dominion over all who have not been, are not, or shall not be reborn from above. This rebirth is wrought by the power of the Holy Ghost creating in the hearts of God's chosen ones an assured faith in the promise of God revealed to us in His Word; by this faith we grasp Christ Jesus with the graces and blessings promised in Him.

CHAPTER IV

THE REVELATION OF THE PROMISE

We constantly believe that God, after the fearful and horrible departure of man from His obedience, did seek Adam again, call upon him, rebuke and convict him of his sin, and in the end made unto him a most joyful promise, that 'the seed of the woman should bruise the head of the serpent', that is, that he should destroy the works of the devil. This promise was repeated and made clearer from time to time; it was embraced with joy, and most constantly received by all the faithful from Adam to Noah, from Noah to Abraham, from Abraham to David, and so onwards to the incarnation of Christ Jesus; all (we mean the believing fathers under the law) did see the joyful day of Christ Jesus, and did rejoice.

CHAPTER V

THE CONTINUANCE, INCREASE AND PRESERVATION
OF THE KIRK

We most surely believe that God preserved, instructed, multiplied, honoured, adorned and called from death to life His Kirk in all ages since Adam until the coming of Christ Jesus in the flesh. For He called Abraham from his father's country, instructed him and multiplied his seed; he marvellously preserved him, and more marvellously delivered his seed from the bondage and tyranny of Pharaoh; to them He gave His laws, constitutions and ceremonies; to them He gave the land of Canaan; after He had given them judges, and afterwards Saul, He gave David to be king, to whom He gave promise that of the fruit of his loins should one sit forever upon his royal throne. To this same people from time to time He sent prophets, to recall them to the right way of their God, from which sometimes they strayed by idolatry. And although, because of their stubborn contempt for righteousness He was compelled to give them into the hands of their enemies, as had previously been threatened by the mouth of Moses, so that the holy city was destroyed, the temple burned with fire, and the whole land desolate for seventy years, yet in mercy He restored them again to Jerusalem, where the city and temple were rebuilt, and they endured against all temptations and assaults of Satan till the Messiah came according to the promise.

Chapter VI

THE INCARNATION OF CHRIST JESUS

When the fullness of time came, God sent His Son, His eternal Wisdom, the substance of His own glory, into this world, who took the nature of humanity from the substance of a woman, a virgin, by means of the Holy Ghost. And so was born the 'just seed of David', the 'Angel of the great counsel of God', the very Messiah promised, whom we confess and acknowledge to be Emmanuel, true God and true man, two perfect natures united and joined in one person. So by our Confession we condemn the damnable and pestilent heresies of Arius, Marcion, Eutyches, Nestorius and such others as did either deny the eternity of His Godhead, or the truth of His humanity, or confounded them, or else divided them.

Chapter VII

WHY THE MEDIATOR HAD TO BE TRUE GOD
AND TRUE MAN

We acknowledge and confess that this wonderful union between the Godhead and the humanity in Christ Jesus did arise from the eternal and immutable decree of God from which all our salvation springs and depends.

Chapter VIII

ELECTION

That same eternal God and Father, who by grace alone chose us in His Son Christ Jesus before the foundation of the world was laid, appointed Him to be our head, our brother, our pastor and the great bishop of our souls. But since the opposition between the justice of God and our sins was such that no flesh by itself could or might have attained unto God, it behoved the Son of God to descend unto us and take Himself a body of our body, flesh of our flesh, and bone of our bone, and so become the Mediator between God and man, giving power to as many as believe in Him to be the sons of God; as He Himself says, 'I ascend to My Father and to your Father, to My God and to your God'. By this most holy brotherhood whatever we have lost in Adam is restored to us again. Therefore we are not afraid to call God our Father, not so much because He has created us, which we have in common with the reprobate, as because He has given unto us His only Son to be our brother, and given us grace to acknowledge and embrace Him as our only Mediator. Further, it behoved the Messiah and Redeemer to be true God and true man, because He was able to undergo the punishment of our transgressions and to present Himself in the presence of His Father's Judgment, as in our stead, to suffer for our transgression and disobedience, and by death to overcome him that was the author of death. But because the Godhead alone could not suffer death, and neither could manhood overcome death, He joined both together in one person, that the weakness of one should suffer and be subject to death – which we had deserved – and the infinite and invincible power of the other, that is, of the Godhead, should triumph, and purchase for us life, liberty and perpetual victory. So we confess, and most undoubtedly believe.

Chapter IX

CHRIST'S DEATH, PASSION AND BURIAL

That our Lord Jesus offered Himself a voluntary sacrifice unto His Father for us, that He suffered contradiction of sinners, that He was wounded and plagued for our transgressions, that He, the clean innocent Lamb of God, was condemned in the presence of an earthly judge, that we should be absolved before the judgment seat of our God; that He suffered not only the cruel death of the cross, which was accursed by the sentence of God; but also that He suffered for a season the wrath of His Father which sinners had deserved. But yet we avow that He remained the only, well beloved and blessed Son of His Father even in the midst of His anguish and torment which He suffered in body and soul to make full atonement for the sins of His people. From this we confess and avow that there remains no other sacrifice for sin; if any affirm so, we do not hesitate to say that they are blasphemers against Christ's death and the everlasting atonement thereby purchased for us.

CHAPTER X

THE RESURRECTION

We undoubtedly believe, since it was impossible that the sorrows of death should retain in bondage the Author of life, that our Lord Jesus crucified, dead and buried, who descended into hell, did rise again for our justification, and the destruction of him who was the author of death, and brought life again to us who were subject to death and its bondage. We know that His resurrection was confirmed by the testimony of His enemies, and by the resurrection of the dead, whose sepulchres did open, and they did rise and appear to many within the city of Jerusalem. It was also confirmed by the testimony of His angels, and by the senses and judgment of His apostles and of others, who had conversation, and did eat and drink with Him after His resurrection.

CHAPTER XI

THE ASCENSION

We do not doubt but that the selfsame body which was born of the virgin, was crucified, dead and buried, and which did rise again, did ascend into the heavens, for the accomplishment of all things, where in our name and for our comfort He has received all power in heaven and earth, where He sits at the right hand of the Father, having received His kingdom, the only advocate and mediator for us. Which glory, honour and prerogative, He alone among the brethren shall possess till all His enemies are made His footstool, as we undoubtedly believe they shall be in the Last Judgment. We believe that the same Lord Jesus shall visibly return for this Last Judgment as He was seen to ascend. And then, we firmly believe, the time of refreshing and restitution of all things shall come, so that those who from the beginning have suffered violence, injury and wrong, for righteousness' sake, shall inherit that blessed immortality promised them from the beginning. But, on the other hand, the stubborn, disobedient, cruel persecutors, filthy persons, idolators and all sorts of the unbelieving, shall be cast into the dungeon of utter darkness, where their worm shall not die, nor their fire be quenched. The remembrance of that day, and of the Judgment to be executed in it, is not only a bridle by which our carnal lusts are restrained but also such inestimable comfort that neither the threatening of worldly princes, nor the fear of present danger or of temporal death, may move us to renounce and forsake that blessed society which we, the members, have with our Head and only Mediator, Christ Jesus: whom we confess and avow to be the promised Messiah, the only Head of His Kirk, our just Lawgiver, our only High Priest, Advocate and Mediator. To which honours and offices, if man or angel presume to intrude themselves, we utterly detest and abhor them, as blasphemous to our sovereign and supreme Governor, Christ Jesus.

CHAPTER XII

FAITH IN THE HOLY GHOST

Our faith and its assurance do not proceed from flesh and blood, that is to say, from natural powers within us, but are the inspiration of the Holy Ghost; whom we confess to be God, equal with the Father and with His Son, who sanctifies us and brings us into all truth by His own working, without whom we should remain forever enemies to God and ignorant of His Son, Christ Jesus. For by nature we are so dead, blind and perverse, that neither can we feel when we are pricked, see the light when it shines, nor assent to the will of God when it is revealed, unless the Spirit of the Lord Jesus quicken that which is dead, remove the darkness from our minds and bow our stubborn hearts to the obedience of His blessed will. And so, as we confess that God the Father created us when we were not, as His Son our Lord Jesus redeemed us when we were enemies to Him, so also do we confess that the Holy Ghost does sanctify and regenerate us, without respect to any merit proceeding from us, be it before or be it after our regeneration. To put this even more plainly; as we willingly disclaim any honour and glory for our own creation and redemption, so do we willingly also for our regeneration and sanctification; for by ourselves we are not capable of thinking one good thought, but He who has begun the work in us alone continues us in it, to the praise and glory of His undeserved grace.

Chapter XIII

THE CAUSE OF GOOD WORKS

The cause of good works, we confess, is not our free will, but the Spirit of the Lord Jesus, who, dwelling in our hearts by true faith, brings forth such works as God has prepared for us to walk in. For we most boldly affirm that it is blasphemy to say that Christ abides in the hearts of those in whom is no spirit of sanctification. Therefore we do not hesitate to affirm that murderers, oppressors, cruel persecutors, adulterers, filthy persons, idolators, drunkards, thieves and all workers of iniquity have neither true faith nor anything of the Spirit of the Lord Jesus, so long as they obstinately continue in wickedness. For as soon as the Spirit of the Lord Jesus, whom God's chosen children receive by true faith, takes possession of the heart of any man, so soon does He regenerate and renew him, so that he begins to hate what before he loved, and to love what he hated before. Thence comes that continual battle which is between the flesh and the Spirit in God's children, while the flesh and the natural man, being corrupt, lust for things pleasant and delightful to themselves, are envious in adversity and proud in prosperity, and every moment prone and ready to offend the majesty of God. But the Spirit of God, who bears witness to our spirit that we are the sons of God, makes us resist filthy pleasures and groan in God's presence for deliverance from this bondage of corruption, and finally to triumph over sin so that it does not reign in our mortal bodies. Other men do not share this conflict since they do not have God's Spirit, but they readily follow and obey sin and feel no regrets, since they act as the devil and their corrupt nature urge. But the sons of God fight against sin; sob and mourn when they find themselves tempted to do evil; and, if they fall, rise again with earnest and unfeigned repentance. They do these things, not by their own power, but by the power of the Lord Jesus, apart from whom they can do nothing.

Chapter XIV

THE WORKS WHICH ARE COUNTED GOOD BEFORE GOD

We confess and acknowledge that God has given to man His holy law, in which not only all such works as displease and offend His godly majesty are forbidden, but also those which please Him and which He has promised to reward are commanded. These works are of two kinds. The one is done to the honour of God, the other to the profit of our neighbour, and both have the revealed will of God as their assurance. To have one God, to worship and honour Him, to call upon Him in all our troubles, to reverence His holy Name, to hear His Word and to believe it, and to share in His holy sacraments, belong to the first kind. To honour father, mother, princes, rulers and superior powers; to love them, to support them, to obey their orders if they are not contrary to the commands of God, to save the lives of the innocent, to repress tyranny, to defend the oppressed, to keep our bodies clean and holy, to live in soberness and temperance, to deal justly with all men in word and deed, and, finally, to repress any desire to harm our neighbour, are the good works of the second kind,

and these are most pleasing and acceptable to God as He
has commanded them Himself. Acts to the contrary are sins,
which always displease Him and provoke Him to anger, such
as, not to call upon Him alone when we have need, not to
hear His Word with reverence, but to condemn and despise
it, to have or worship idols, to maintain and defend idolatry,
lightly to esteem the reverend name of God, to profane, abuse
or condemn the sacraments of Christ Jesus, to disobey or
resist any whom God has placed in authority, so long as
they do not exceed the bounds of their office, to murder, or
to consent thereto, to bear hatred, or to let innocent blood
be shed if we can prevent it. In conclusion, we confess and
affirm that the breach of any other commandment of the first
or second kind is sin, by which God's anger and displeasure
are kindled against the proud, unthankful world. So that
we affirm good works to be those alone which are done in
faith and at the command of God who, in His law, has set
forth the things that please Him. We affirm that evil works
are not only those expressly done against God's command,
but also, in religious matters and the worship of God, those
things which have no other warrant than the invention and
opinion of man. From the beginning God has rejected such,
as we learn from the words of the prophet Isaiah and of our
master, Christ Jesus, 'In vain do they worship Me, teaching
the doctrines and commandments of men'.

Chapter XV

THE PERFECTION OF THE LAW
AND THE IMPERFECTION OF MAN

We confess and acknowledge that the law of God is most
just, equal, holy and perfect, commanding those things
which, when perfectly done, can give life and bring man
to eternal felicity; but our nature is so corrupt, weak and
imperfect that we are never able perfectly to fulfil the works
of the law. Even after we are reborn, if we say that we have
no sin, we deceive ourselves and the truth of God is not in
us. It is therefore essential for us to lay hold on Christ Jesus,
in His righteousness and His atonement, since He is the end

and consummation of the Law and since it is by Him that we are set at liberty so that the curse of God may not fall upon us, even though we do not fulfil the Law in all points. For as God the Father beholds us in the body of His Son Christ Jesus, He accepts our imperfect obedience as if it were perfect, and covers our works, which are defiled with many stains, with the righteousness of His Son. We do not mean that we are so set at liberty that we owe no obedience to the Law – for we have already acknowledged its place – but we affirm that no man on earth, with the sole exception of Christ Jesus, has given, gives or shall give in action that obedience to the Law which the Law requires. When we have done all things, we must fall down and unfeignedly confess that we are unprofitable servants. Therefore, whoever boasts of the merits of his own works, or puts his trust in works of supererogation, boasts of what does not exist, and puts his trust in damnable idolatry.

CHAPTER XVI

THE KIRK

As we believe in one God, Father, Son and Holy Ghost, so we firmly believe that from the beginning there has been, now is, and to the end of the world shall be, one Kirk, that is to say, one company and multitude of men chosen by God, who rightly worship and embrace Him by true faith in Christ Jesus, who is the only Head of the Kirk, even as it is the body and spouse of Christ Jesus. This Kirk is Catholic, that is, universal, because it contains the chosen of all ages, of all realms, nations and tongues, be they of the Jews or be they of the Gentiles, who have communion and society with God the Father, and with His Son, Christ Jesus, through the sanctification of His Holy Spirit. It is therefore called the communion, not of profane persons, but of saints, who, as citizens of the heavenly Jerusalem, have the fruit of inestimable benefits, one God, one Lord Jesus, one faith and one baptism. Out of this Kirk there is neither life nor eternal felicity. Therefore we utterly abhor the blasphemy of those who hold that men who live according to equity and justice shall be saved, no matter what religion they profess. For since there is neither life nor salvation without Christ Jesus, so shall none have part therein but those whom the Father has given unto His Son Christ Jesus, and those who in time come to Him, avow His doctrine and believe in Him. (We include the children with the believing parents.) This Kirk is invisible, known only to God, who alone knows whom He has chosen, and includes both the chosen who are departed, the Kirk triumphant, those who yet live and fight against sin and Satan, and those who shall live hereafter.

Chapter XVII

THE IMMORTALITY OF SOULS

The chosen departed are in peace, and rest from their labours; not that they sleep and are lost in oblivion as some fanatics hold, for they are delivered from all fear and torment, and all the temptations to which we and all God's chosen are subject in this life, and because of which we are called the Kirk Militant. On the other hand, the reprobate and unfaithful departed have anguish, torment and pain which cannot be expressed. Neither the one nor the other is in such sleep that they feel no joy or torment, as is testified by Christ's parable in St Luke 16, His words to the thief, and the words of the souls crying under the altar, 'O Lord, Thou that art righteous and just, how long shalt Thou not revenge our blood upon those that dwell in the earth?'

Chapter XVIII

THE NOTES BY WHICH THE TRUE KIRK SHALL BE DETERMINED FROM THE FALSE, AND WHO SHALL BE JUDGE OF DOCTRINE

Since Satan has laboured from the beginning to adorn his pestilent synagogue with the title of the Kirk of God, and has incited cruel murderers to persecute, trouble and molest the true Kirk and its members, as Cain did to Abel, Ishmael to Isaac, Esau to Jacob, and the whole priesthood of the Jews to Christ Jesus Himself and His apostles after Him, so it is essential that the true Kirk be distinguished from the filthy synagogues by clear and perfect notes lest we, being deceived, receive and embrace, to our own condemnation, the one for the other. The notes, signs and assured tokens whereby the spotless bride of Christ is known from the horrible harlot, the false Kirk, we state, are neither antiquity, usurped title, lineal succession, appointed place nor the numbers of men approving an error. For Cain was before Abel and Seth in age and title; Jerusalem had precedence above all other parts of the earth, for in it were priests lineally descended from Aaron, and greater numbers followed the scribes, pharisees and priests than unfeignedly believed and followed Christ Jesus and His doctrine . . . and yet no man of judgment, we suppose, will hold that any of the forenamed were the Kirk of God. The notes of the true Kirk, therefore, we believe, confess and avow to be: first, the true preaching of the Word of God, in which God has revealed Himself to us, as the writings of the prophets and apostles declare; secondly, the right administration of the sacraments of Christ Jesus, with which must be associated the Word and promise of God to seal and confirm them in our hearts; and lastly, ecclesiastical discipline uprightly ministered, as God's Word prescribes, whereby vice is repressed and virtue nourished. Then wherever these notes are seen and continue for any time, be the number complete or not, there, beyond any doubt, is the true Kirk of Christ, who, according to His promise, is in its midst. This is not that universal Kirk of which we have spoken before, but particular Kirks, such as were in Corinth, Galatia, Ephesus and other places where the ministry was planted by Paul and which he himself called Kirks of God. Such Kirks, we the inhabitants of the realm of Scotland confessing Christ Jesus do claim to have in our cities, towns and reformed districts because of the doctrine taught in our Kirks, contained in the written Word of God, that is, the Old and New Testaments, in those books which were originally reckoned canonical. We affirm that in these all things necessary to be believed for the salvation of man are sufficiently expressed. The interpretation of Scripture, we confess, does not belong to any private or public person, nor yet to any Kirk for pre-eminence or precedence, personal or local, which it has above others, but pertains to the Spirit of God by whom the Scriptures were written. When controversy arises about the right understanding of any passage or sentence of Scripture, or for the reformation of any abuse within the Kirk of God, we ought not so much to ask what men have said or done before us, as what the Holy Ghost uniformly speaks within the body of the Scriptures and what Christ Jesus Himself did and commanded. For it is agreed by all that the Spirit of God, who is the Spirit of unity, cannot contradict Himself. So if the interpretation or opinion of any theologian, Kirk, or council, is contrary to the plain Word of God written in any other passage of the Scripture, it is most certain that this is not the true understanding and meaning of the Holy Ghost, although councils, realms and nations have approved and received it. We dare not receive or admit any interpretation which is contrary to any principal point of our faith, or to any other plain text of Scripture, or to the rule of love.

Chapter XIX
THE AUTHORITY OF THE SCRIPTURES

As we believe and confess the Scriptures of God sufficient to instruct and make perfect the man of God, so do we affirm and avow their authority to be from God, and not to depend on men or angels. We affirm, therefore, that those who say the Scriptures have no other authority save that which they have received from the Kirk are blasphemous against God and injurious to the true Kirk, which always hears and obeys the voice of her own Spouse and Pastor, but takes not upon her to be mistress over the same.

Chapter XX
GENERAL COUNCILS, THEIR POWER, AUTHORITY
AND THE CAUSE OF THEIR SUMMONING

As we do not rashly condemn what good men, assembled together in General Councils lawfully gathered, have set before us, so we do not receive uncritically whatever has been declared to men under the name of the General Councils, for it is plain that, being human, some of them have manifestly erred, and that in matters of great weight and importance. So far then as the Council confirms its decrees by the plain Word of God, so far do we reverence and embrace them. But if men, under the name of a Council, pretend to forge for us new articles of faith, or to make decisions contrary to the Word of God, then we must utterly deny them as the doctrine of devils, drawing our souls from the voice of the one God to follow the doctrines and teachings of men. The reason why the General Councils met was not to make any permanent law which God had not made before, nor yet to form new articles for our belief, nor to give the Word of God authority; much less to make that to be His Word, or even the true interpretation of it, which was not expressed previously by His holy will in His Word; but the reason for Councils, at least of those that deserve that name, was partly to refute heresies, and to give public confession of their faith to the generations following, which they did by the authority of God's written Word, and not by any opinion or prerogative that they could not err by reason of their numbers. This, we judge, was the primary reason for General Councils. The second was that good policy and order should be constituted and observed in the Kirk where, as in the house of God, it becomes all things to be done decently and in order. Not that we think any policy or order of ceremonies can be appointed for all ages, times and places; for as ceremonies which men have devised are but temporal, so they may, and ought to be, changed, when they foster superstition rather than edify the Kirk.

CHAPTER XXI

THE SACRAMENTS

As the fathers under the Law, besides the reality of the sacrifices, had two chief sacraments, that is, circumcision and the passover, and those who rejected these were not reckoned among God's people, so do we acknowledge and confess that now in the time of the Gospel we have two chief sacraments, which alone were instituted by the Lord Jesus and commanded to be used by all who will be counted members of His body, that is, Baptism and the Supper or Table of the Lord Jesus, also called the Communion of His Body and Blood. These sacraments, both of the Old Testament and of the New, were instituted by God not only to make a visible distinction between His people and those who were without the Covenant, but also to exercise the faith of His children and, by participation of these sacraments, to seal in their hearts the assurance of His promise, and of that most blessed conjunction, union and society which the chosen have with their Head, Christ Jesus. And so we utterly condemn the vanity of those who affirm the sacraments to be nothing else than naked and bare signs. No, we assuredly believe that by Baptism we are engrafted into Christ Jesus, to be made partakers of His righteousness, by which our sins are covered and remitted, and also that in the Supper rightly used, Christ Jesus is so joined with us that He becomes the very nourishment and food of our souls. Not that we imagine any transubstantiation of bread into Christ's body, and of wine into His natural blood, as the Romanists have perniciously taught and wrongly believed; but this union and conjunction which we have with the body and blood of Christ Jesus in the right use of the sacraments is wrought by means of the Holy Ghost, who by true faith carries us above all things that are visible, carnal and earthly, and makes us feed upon the body and blood of Christ Jesus, once broken and shed for us but now in heaven, and appearing for us in the presence of His Father. Notwithstanding the distance between His glorified body in heaven and mortal men on earth, yet we must assuredly believe that the bread which we break is the communion of Christ's body and the cup which we bless the communion of His blood. Thus we confess and believe without doubt that the faithful, in the right use of the Lord's Table, do so eat the body and drink the blood of the Lord Jesus that He remains in them and they in Him; they are so made flesh of His flesh and bone of His bone that as the eternal Godhood has given to the flesh of Christ Jesus, which by nature was corruptible and mortal, life and immortality, so the eating and drinking of the flesh and blood of Christ Jesus does the like for us. We grant that this is neither given to us merely at the time nor by the power and virtue of the sacrament alone, but we affirm that the faithful, in the right use of the Lord's Table, have such union with Christ Jesus as the natural man cannot apprehend. Further we affirm that although the faithful, hindered by negligence and human weakness, do not profit as much as they ought in the actual moment of the Supper, yet afterwards it shall bring forth fruit, being living seed sown in good ground; for the Holy Spirit, who can never be separated from the right institution of the Lord Jesus, will not deprive the faithful of the fruit of that mystical action. Yet all this, we say again, comes of that true faith which apprehends Christ Jesus, who alone makes the sacrament effective in us. Therefore, if anyone slanders us by saying that we affirm or believe the sacraments to be symbols and nothing more, they are libellous and speak against the plain facts. On the other hand we readily admit that we make a distinction between Christ Jesus in His eternal substance and the elements of the sacramental signs. So we neither worship the elements, in place of that which they signify, nor yet do we despise them or undervalue them, but we use them with great reverence, examining ourselves diligently before we participate, since we are assured by the mouth of the apostle that 'whosoever shall eat this bread, and drink this cup of the Lord, unworthily, shall be guilty of the body and blood of the Lord'.

Chapter XXII

THE RIGHT ADMINISTRATION OF THE SACRAMENTS

Two things are necessary for the right administration of the sacraments. The first is that they should be ministered by lawful ministers, and we declare that these are men appointed to preach the Word, unto whom God has given the power to preach the Gospel, and who are lawfully called by some Kirk. The second is that they should be ministered in the elements and manner which God has appointed. Otherwise they cease to be the sacraments of Christ Jesus. This is why we abandon the teaching of the Roman Church and withdraw from its sacraments; firstly, because their ministers are not true ministers of Christ Jesus (indeed they even allow women, whom the Holy Ghost will not permit to preach in the congregation, to baptise) and, secondly, because they have so adulterated both the sacraments with their own additions that no part of Christ's original act remains in its original simplicity. The addition of oil, salt, spittle and such like in baptism are merely human additions. To adore or venerate the sacrament, to carry it through streets and towns in procession, or to reserve it in a special case, is not the proper use of Christ's sacrament but an abuse of it. Christ Jesus said, 'Take ye, eat ye', and 'Do this in remembrance of Me'. By these words and commands He sanctified bread and wine to be the sacrament of His holy body and blood, so that the one should be eaten and that all should drink of the other, and not that they should be reserved for worship or honoured as God, as the Romanists do. Further, in withdrawing one part of the sacrament – the blessed cup – from the people, they have committed sacrilege. Moreover, if the sacraments are to be rightly used it is essential that the end and purpose of their institution should be understood, not only by the minister but by the recipients. For if the recipient does not understand what is being done, the sacrament is not being rightly used, as is seen in the case of the Old Testament sacrifices. Similarly, if the teacher teaches false doctrine which is hateful to God, even though the sacraments are His own ordinance, they are not rightly used, since wicked men have used them for another end than what God commanded. We affirm that this has been done to the sacraments in the Roman Church, for there the whole action of the Lord Jesus is adulterated in form, purpose and meaning. What Christ Jesus did, and commanded to be done, is evident from the Gospels and from St Paul; what the priest does at the altar we do not need to tell. The end and purpose of Christ's institution, for which it should be used, is set forth in the words, 'Do this in remembrance of Me', and 'For as often as ye eat this bread and drink this cup ye do show' – that is, extol, preach, magnify and praise – 'the Lord's death, till He come'. But let the words of the mass, and their own doctors and teachings witness, what is the purpose and meaning of the mass; it is that, as mediators between Christ and His Kirk, they should offer to God the Father a sacrifice in propitiation for the sins of the living and of the dead. This doctrine is blasphemous to Christ Jesus and would deprive His unique sacrifice, once offered on the cross for the cleansing of all who are to be sanctified, of its sufficiency; so we detest and renounce it.

Chapter XXIII

TO WHOM SACRAMENTS APPERTAIN

We hold that baptism applies as much to the children of the faithful as to those who are of age and discretion, and so we condemn the error of the Anabaptists, who deny that children should be baptised before they have faith and understanding. But we hold that the Supper of the Lord is only for those who are of the household of faith and can try and examine themselves both in their faith and their duty to their neighbours. Those who eat and drink at that holy table without faith, or without peace and goodwill to their brethren, eat unworthily. This is the reason why ministers in our Kirk make public and individual examination of those who are to be admitted to the table of the Lord Jesus.

Chapter XXIV

THE CIVIL MAGISTRATE

We confess and acknowledge that empires, kingdoms, dominions and cities are appointed and ordained by God; the powers and authorities in them, emperors in empires, kings in their realms, dukes and princes in their dominions, and magistrates in cities, are ordained by God's holy ordinance for the manifestation of His own glory and for the good and well being of all men. We hold that any men who conspire to rebel or to overturn the civil powers, as duly established, are not merely enemies to humanity but rebels against God's will. Further, we confess and acknowledge that such persons as are set in authority are to be loved, honoured, feared and held in the highest respect, because they are the lieutenants of God, and in their councils God Himself doth sit and judge. They are the judges and princes to whom God has given the sword for the praise and defence of good men and the punishment of all open evil doers. Moreover, we state that the preservation and purification of religion is particularly the duty of kings, princes, rulers and magistrates. They are not only appointed for civil government but also to maintain true religion and to suppress all idolatry and superstition. This may be seen in David, Jehosaphat, Hezekiah, Josiah and others highly commended for their zeal in that cause.

Therefore we confess and avow that those who resist the supreme powers, so long as they are acting in their own spheres, are resisting God's ordinance and cannot be held guiltless. We further state that so long as princes and rulers vigilantly fulfil their office, anyone who denies them aid, counsel or service denies it to God, who by His lieutenant craves it of them.

Chapter XXV

THE GIFTS FREELY GIVEN TO THE KIRK

Although the Word of God truly preached, the Sacraments rightly ministered, and discipline executed according to the Word of God, are certain and infallible signs of the true Kirk, we do not mean that every individual person in that company is a chosen member of Christ Jesus. We acknowledge and confess that many weeds and tares are sown among the corn and grow in great abundance in its midst, and that the reprobate may be found in the fellowship of the chosen and may take an outward part with them in the benefits of the Word and sacraments. But since they only confess God for a time with their mouths and not with their hearts, they lapse and do not continue to the end. Therefore they do not share the fruits of Christ's death, resurrection and ascension. But such as unfeignedly believe with the heart and boldly confess the Lord Jesus with their mouths shall certainly receive His gifts. Firstly, in this life, they shall receive remission of sins and that by faith in Christ's blood alone; for though sin shall remain and continually abide in our mortal bodies, yet it shall not be counted against us, but be pardoned and covered with Christ's righteousness. Secondly, in the general judgment, there shall be given to every man and woman resurrection of the flesh. The sea shall give up her dead, and the earth those who are buried within her. Yea, the Eternal, our God, shall stretch out His hand on the dust, and the dead shall arise incorruptible, and in the very substance of the selfsame flesh which every man now bears, to receive according to their works, glory or punishment. Such as now delight in vanity, cruelty, filthiness, superstition or idolatry shall be condemned to the fire unquenchable, in which those who now serve the devil in all abominations shall be tormented forever, both in body and in spirit. But such as continue in welldoing to the end, boldly confessing the Lord Jesus, shall receive glory, honour and immortality, we constantly believe, to reign forever in life everlasting with Christ Jesus, to whose glorified body all His chosen shall be made like, when He shall appear again in judgment and shall render up the Kingdom to God His Father, who then shall be and ever shall remain, all in all things, God blessed forever. To whom, with the Son and the Holy Ghost, be all honour and glory, now and ever. Amen.

Arise, O Lord, and let Thine enemies be confounded; let them flee from Thy presence that hate Thy godly Name. Give Thy servants strength to speak Thy Word with boldness, and let all nations cleave to the true knowledge of Thee. Amen.

These Acts and articles were read in the face of the
Parliament and ratified by the Three Estates,
at Edinburgh the 17 day of August,
the year of God 1560 years.